Contents

Volume 101:2 Summer 2011

Centrefold

Reviews

EDITORIAL

FIONA SAMPSON

Journalists sometimes ask, *Why aren't today's poets politically engaged?* or, *Where are the contemporary war poets?* Yet everyone who has read John Agard or Jackie Kay, Grace Nichols or Carol Ann Duffy for GCSE English will be aware that contemporary British poetry explores questions of identity, authority and social rights. These questions are unmistakably political. In 2011 poets are continuing these explorations, though sometimes, perhaps, using less declarative forms. For example it is still a political as well as a poetic act for a woman poet to dare to entertain philosophical or metaphysical ideas; or for poets with rich, hyphenated cultural backgrounds to write in forms which owe something to whatever part of that background transgresses traditional British lyric boundaries. In this sense, of not selling out, poets like Mimi Khalvati, with her use of hieratic, Persian-derived poetics, Gwyneth Lewis and Menna Elfyn (*women* writing in Welsh and using non-traditional "foreign" forms), and the emerging generation of the *Ten* anthology are all political poets.

In other words, politics might not be just potential subject matter, but part of a poetic *project*, sliding onto and off the page. The Poetry Translation Centre team, led by Sarah Maguire, are engaged in just such a project: they produce beautifully-translated texts, but they are acting to shift the range of poetic voices available to British readers, and so our collective cultural understanding. Then there are the protagonists like Maureen Duffy, who helped win us Public Lending Right, whose work for the collective good runs alongside their own writing, as does that of those who edit and publish, those who deliver writing in health care and prisons, and – moving still further from the page – poets like Ian Duhig, who works in social housing.

Which is not to say that Sean O'Brien's *cante jondo* for post-industrial Britain, or even that refusal to disavow contemporary, urban, working-class culture which marked out many young male poets in the 1990s (Don Paterson, Paul Farley, Neil Rollinson), is anything less than profoundly political and poetic. But it does suggest that the political "follows us around". In a country in which, at present, armed conflict is off-shore and there is no draft, most poets are lucky enough to have no first-hand experience of war. It's arguably impossible to write well enough to honour a tragic experience one that hasn't had, and maybe distasteful to try: no poetry after Auschwitz. Our politics reveal themselves, though, in how we write and act right where we are.

CONTRIBUTORS

Dejan Bogojević is a poet and editor from Valjevo, Serbia. **John Burnside**'s *Black Cat Bone* (Cape) appears in August. **Aviva Dautch**'s poems have appeared in *Agenda, Modern Poetry in Translation* and *The Long Poem Magazine.* **Caroline Clark**'s poems and essays have appeared in *Agenda, The Reader, The Interpreter's House, The Malahat Review* etc. **Claire Crowther**'s latest publication is *Incense* (Flarestack). **Maureen Duffy** has published thirty-one books, is President of Honour of the British Copyright Council and Authors' Lending and Copyright Society and a Vice President of the RSL. **Ian Duhig**'s *Pandorama* (Picador, 2010) is reviewed in this issue. He is writer in residence at this year's Ledbury Festival, the context for 'Skew Sonnets'. **Roger Garfitt**'s *The Horseman's Word* is just published by Jonathan Cape. **Philip Gross** won the T.S. Eliot Prize 2009; *Deep Field* is due from Bloodaxe (Nov 2011). **Marilyn Hacker** has received both the PEN Award for Poetry in Translation and the PEN/Voelcker Award for Poetry. **David Harsent**'s *Night* (Faber, Jan), is a PBS Choice and shortlisted for the T.S. Eliot Prize. **Mimi Khalvati**'s *The Meanest Flower* was shortlisted for the T.S. Eliot Prize 2007. Her *New & Selected Poems* is forthcoming from Carcanet. **John Kinsella**'s *Armour* is due out with Picador in November. He is a Fellow of Churchill College and a Professorial Research Fellow at the University of Western Australia. **Lan Lan**, b. Shandong 1967 and currently residing in Beijing, is a national award-winning Chinese poet. **Gwyneth Lewis** was National Poet of Wales 2005-06. Her most recent book is *Sparrow Tree*. **Tim Liardet**'s *The Storm House* (Carcanet) appears in June. *The Blood Choir* was shortlisted for the T.S. Eliot Prize 2006. **Sarah Maguire**'s *The Pomegranates of Kandahar* was shortlisted for the T.S. Eliot Prize 2007. **Maitreyabandhu** has won the Keats-Shelley, Basil Bunting, Geoffrey Dearmer and Ledbury Festival prizes. **Jamie McKendrick**'s latest books are *Crocodiles and Obelisks* (Faber, 2007) and his 2010 edition of Valerio Magrelli, which won the Weidenfeld Translation Prize. **Ian McMillan** is a poet and broadcaster who presents *The Verb*: Friday nights, BBC R3. **Duncan Stewart Muir** grew up in the Scottish Hebrides and currently lives in Manchuria, China, where he working on his first novel. **Michael Murphy**'s last publications, both in 2008, were a collection, *Allotments,* and his edition of *The Collected Poems of Kenneth Allott*. **Daljit Nagra** won the Forward First Collection Prize for *Look We Have Coming To Dover*. **Knut Ødegård** is one of Norway's best known poets and founder of the Bjørnson festival. He is also the Consul General for Macedonia in Norway. **Ruth Padel**'s *Darwin: A life in poems* (Chatto, 2009) was shortlisted for the Costa Poetry Prize. **Neil Rollinson**'s latest collection is *Demolition* (Cape, 2008). **Omar Sabbagh**'s debut, *My Only Ever Oedipal Complaint,* is reviewed in this issue. His second collection, *The Square Root of Beirut,* is forthcoming (Feb 2012). **Denise Saul**'s *White Narcissi* (2007) was a PBS Pamphlet Choice. **Alan Stubbs** was commended in the Arvon and shortlisted in the Bridport prizes. **Fiona Sze-Lorrain**, author of *Water the Moon* (Marick Press, 2010), is a co-editor of Cerise Press who writes and translates in English, French and Chinese. **Adam Thorpe**'s *Bird with a Broken Wing* was Forward shortlisted in 2007. **Sarah Wardle**'s *A Knowable World* appeared in 2009. **Ben Wilkinson** was shortlisted for the Picador Poetry Prize earlier this year.

POEMS

O, how ravishingly slow.

– *Caroline Clark*

Mimi Khalvati
The Blanket

Cold, yes, under a sodium sky at three o'clock in the morning.
But there's this shawl to wear and tea with Manuka honey.

And across the only gap in the border, a thousand refugees an hour
pouring through Ras al-Jedir. An hour? By morning, my morning,

another five thousand, by lunchtime, another five and how many
have even a striped hemp blanket? Fifteen thousand blankets!

Imagine one. The way it folds stiffly as a tent around the head
bent back, the shoulders jutting, knees drawn up, wrists free,

the lone triangular edifice. Feel the weave. Hairy, ridged.
Smell it. Determine the sightlines either side of the hollowed cheeks.

Imagine the scene in silence, not as it would be. The blanket
as a block, a wood carving. The tools: straight gouge, spoon gouge,

back bent, dog leg, fishtail chisels, V-tools, punches, vices;
hook knives, drawknives, rasps and rifflers, mallets, saws, abrasives;

slip waterstones – how quiet they sound – and strops for sharpening.
Figure in a blanket. In acacia, sycamore or, most likely, olive.

The Swarm

Snow was literally swarming round the streetlamp like gnats.
The closer they came, the larger they grew, snow-gnats, snow-bees,

and in my snood, smoking in the snow, I watched them.
Everyone else was behind the door, I could hear their noise

which made the snow, the swarm, more silent. More welcome.
I could have watched for hours and seen nothing more than specks

against the light interrupting light and away from it, flying blind
but carrying light, specks becoming atoms. They flew too fast

to become snow itself, flying in a random panic, looming close
but disappearing, like flakes on the tongue, at the point of recognition.

They died as they landed, riding on their own melting as poems do
and in the morning there was nothing to be seen of them.

Instead, a streak of lemon, lemon honey, ringed the sky
but the cloud-lid never lifted, the weekend promised a blizzard.

I could have watched for hours and seen nothing more than I do now,
an image, metaphor, but not the blind imperative that drove them.

Jamie McKendrick
Azurite

It's azurite, he said, makes the pool blue.
A green-tinged blue Venetian artists used
for painting sea, keeping lapis lazuli
for their hazy, angel-haunted skies.
We'd driven out to the ramshackle farm,
where the farmer's son had filled a paddock
with scrapped cars as a commercial sideline,
to find your dented Audi a replacement door.

You'd have thought the pool might have given him
pause, with the pride he took in it, might have made
him wonder whether that seepage of oil,
those rusting wrecks were its best protection.
It was like Paul Nash's aircraft graveyard,
all lunar mashed metallic celery,
but that was wartime Cowley 1940,
this the gorse-flecked Ridgeway

a decade ago. So now I've forgotten
how to get there and if you ever got the door
though I remember the pool's oblivious blue,
how I scooped up a chill palmful
surprised it was colourless and how
speckled trout all facing an invisible altar
hung in the uplift, their eyes unlidded,
while the azure current coiled about them.

When I call on you, drained, bandaged, far removed
from any words, from the craft that
you've lifted up and left your mark on,
I lapse into silence and stare at
the tumbled lump of malachite that's been
lying on your garden table – its seams of green
are what azurite becomes when exposed
to air, black-banded but still bright as life.

Lan Lan
Only...

Only night belongs to dreams.
Only still poplars
cattle chewing in a barn trough
only the humming waltz of noon bees –

The listen of spring water. A fixed fire gaze.
Only the storm of one's light footsteps.
Coarse tree barks will part, sealed
     in a bosom –

Only curtains drummed by wind...
Only hushed waters beneath a draft paper
where the universe, its endless mountains sleep –

Concerning Scenery

A series of summits rushing by. A sprinting
forest of locust trees. Field. Field
this scenery is upheld by words
rising. While "fruit"
hangs in mid-sky.

That isn't true. A strange dream
soars over rivers and grasses
dyed green by my ink... But this
vague language's lips and teeth can touch it
giving me all the life of this earth
the taste of a red currant

Translated by Fiona Sze-Lorrain

Denise Saul
Leaving Abyssinia

A foghorn sounds: I notice the distance
between houses and the shore
as the ship pulls away from a pillar:
strata of limestone, clay and granite.
A wall of fog drifts towards the coast;
gulls peck at moss behind a stone ledge.
I sit in a cabin without windows,
unable to tell if I'm moving or not.

I cannot hear what grandfather shouts
from the pier – goodbye – perhaps.
The wind billows in the smell of mackerel.
At night, nothing is certain when I leave
this land where morning and night
come so close together that fishermen
who return boats at sunset hail
those who sail theirs out at dawn.

An hour later, the clock ticks the same way.
It's 1.30 a.m. and as I'm still
awake, I light an oil-lamp to read a book.
I packed books which were needed:
World Dress by Frances Burnett,
Oxford English Reference Dictionary
and *Greek Myths* by Robert Graves.

Here, there is *no* Odysseus to let passengers know
that the ship's motion is 'uniform'.
I recall that phrase from a lesson at school
as that formula was rote learnt:
every body continues... in its state
of rest or of uniform motion... in a right line
unless it is compelled... to change
that state by forces impressed upon it.
I leaf through the story of the Clashing Rocks;
all the sun returns to the underworld.

Tim Liardet
Deleted Scene (The Jug)

You'll never understand why your stepfather pressed you
to fill the jug with water to its fat lip,

those pale Chinese figures painted around its hips
ending the story only so it could begin again.

You listened through chin-length hair, the stepson
staring at the jug with a look which shifted quickly

between embarrassed, helpless and terrified—
You'll never understand why he asked you then

to smash the jug without spilling any water, break it,
he said, any way you want, but do not spill a drop.

You hugged its weight against you, felt water
slop down your shirt and onto your bare feet, let go—

when it smashed on the tiles into exploding bits
and flew everywhere as if somehow in slo-mo,

just for the briefest second the water held
a miraculous jug-shape and stood there on its own—

it trembled, trembled, as you willed it to—
before its hips broadened, brought it slapping to the tiles

and splinters of china sprouted from your palms.
My hands, you said. My jug, he said, *my jug.*

Porte Ouverte On Francophonie: *Marilyn Hacker*

Rachida Madani
from Tales Of A Severed Head

X

She has barricaded herself for she knows
how the desert betrays.
She makes an hourglass of it
and lays her neck where the last
crystal grain will fall.
Waiting, she places a mine
into each poem she launches
without knowing what forehead it will burst
before the word
in her mouth is taken back from her.

XII

Time passes and takes away
half her face
while the other keeps
so few words
so few images
that she can not even write
a pauper's book.
So little saliva that her voice
dries out and breaks
on arid scraping.
Lost now, the dream of howling seas
that besieged the jade palace,
lost through the spell of wishing
long life and wealth

to Shahrayar.
She can no longer set off
following the renegades
she can no longer move forward
she can not say if this hurts her.
She no longer knows if she gropes forward by writing
or if words hurl themselves in her face
she no longer knows with what staff to dig into
what space.
She writes blindly
and fear accompanies her.

XIV

So the gulf will be wider
wolves' howling in
                    love's fissures.
Just as well that you cast
                    layers of silence
into the speeches whispered
                    in the moonlight,
just as well that I stretched barbed wire
between you and me
but I don't know how these poems
splattered with your blood
have come one by one
                    to pierce me.

It is true that the wind increases
                    solitudes
that nostalgia hoists itself up
                    to the dune's peak
and that fields of love grow
in the midst of nettles.
But it hurts me to call to you
with embittered writing
where anger takes over and makes me sister

> to a hurricane
> to lose you between the lines
> that inflict on you the sight of
> > my gashed skin
> your ruins and my defeats.
> It hurts me to find us
> with knives drawn in the arteries
> of this already
> > distant city
> where rending us apart
> has left me
> out of reach of
> > new beginnings.
> But this is my way from now on
> I need not spare you
> in the clamor of the market-place
> prey to madness
> in the thunder of truths
> > spat out at last.
> I do not need to spare you
> we will love each other later...
> Much later
> in the ashes
> > of the crystal palace.

Translated by Marilyn Hacker

Rachida Madani was born in Tangiers, Morocco, in 1951, and still lives there. She was a youthful political militant who expressed her resistance with texts rather than slogans: the poems of her first collection, *Femme je suis*, were read by political prisoners, and the book was prefaced by the poet-militant Abdellatif La'abi, now resident in France; *Contes d'une tête tranchée*, from which this sequence of extracts is taken, is her second book of poems. It was published in Morocco by Editions Al-forkane in 2001. A collection of her poems, including this sequence, was published in Paris by Les Editions de la Différence in 2007, followed by a prose narrative, *L'Histoire peut attendre*.

In *Contes d'une tête tranchée*, Rachida Madani's modern-day Sheherazade is still fighting for her own life and the lives of her fellow citizens. But in the twenty-first century, the threat comes as much from official corruption, denial of human rights, poverty and the detritus of colonialism as from the power still wielded by individual men.

Duncan Stewart Muir
La Santa, Lanzarote

My sister slips into the sea of a quiet dawn,
pulls her body up the coast, until only faint splashes
and the ruffled commotion of rising gulls
identify her stroke, silver in the sun.

In the morning mist, Tinajo's houses
are blurred like snow or ash on the foothills
of the volcano. The birds resettle
on the water, preening away their affront.

Workmen make the most of morning,
of the sun's easy early light,
trading small talk with one another,
and soft low laughter; and the short sound –

of the nail gun with the opposite shore.
A man stalks into the lagoon, lunges
into the water, swims butterfly to the other side,
then lies, chest heaving, glistening

on the sand, content with his short effort.
When she returns, her silver splashes cast up
another white flutter from the surface:
wings beating the sun's rays

into flashes of light, brighter than dawn,
she emerges from the sea, breathing easily,
smiling wide, as if she has just swum, then stalked,
from her own world, into another.

Claire Crowther
Requisition At Abinger

By ponds damming the Tillingbourne
he strikes a bell with his hammer.

By ponds damming the Tillingbourne
hammer men make chains and hooks

on this common land, disparked
to give wood for the mills. My love

(whose need I am going to supply)
is in the first stages of sainthood –

God is giving him things... I'm such
a thing, a bunch of watercress,

more stalk than leaf. The painted smith
opens the clock to sound me out.

He strikes a bell with his hammer.

A note on form:
These two poems are part of a long elegy and are examples of the *fatras*, a fourteenth-century Northern French form that originated in the *fatrasie*, a thirteenth-century nonsense poem. Both *fatrasie* and *fatras* have eleven lines and the *fatras* includes an initial couplet comprised of first and last lines of the eleven. 'Psalm' is a double *fatras* that inverts and re-presents the initial couplet to introduce a second set of eleven lines. Medieval examples of the form also offer rhyme schemes and syllabic rules that I haven't used in these poems.

Psalm

Face, that carries the set and reset of his head,
bear this without a headache.

Face, that carries the set and reset of his head,
steer by it.

Where does his face finish?
It falls out and is absorbed by a razed boundary.

His face is a thumbprint on the topside of my neck.
Alone, my face practises signs as itself.

His face is at the mercy of my head.
It must be hung down sometimes
or thrown back.
It must be swung round and round and
bear this without a headache.

Bear this without a headache,
face that carries the set and reset of his head.

Bear this without a headache.
Surf the sea-sized face that crystallised
after his death. Start at the jaw,
fly to the bow of the upper lip,
crown at the prow of the nose.
Hold the wave of the size of his dissolution
through each tunnel of eye.

Drenched in his mind, the left side of my brain
solves him while the right
dissolves into his vast
face, that carries the set and reset of his head.

Alan Stubbs
a philosophical provocation

this tree is both an assertion and a dialogue
it is ambiguous and playfully sets out in branches
it is rooting too slowly to appreciate in inches
it is not just itself but also lichens and mosses
aggregate on its surfaces, and the spine of trunk
is a book of record in a way, and the flat leaf
a translator of light and air and water, a sheath
of cares where a slaughter of aphids turn gunk
and tear into a million chews, or that tree frogs
may choose to hide beneath and snooze, or foxes
paw at when they parachute loose, and so this
is an interpretation, and that is all it is, a mis-
heard call, a faint echo, an accumulation of
words sighing like leaves on a tree, or a stove
that is ready to cook the meal that's inside it.
This door is blind shut and we don't know it's lit.

Guillevic
A Nail

Only a little rust
on the nail.

It can't have been used yet.
It was taking it easy
like you or me.

It's one of those who have
gone quiet, gone
to look into themselves.

Translated by Roger Garfitt

Maitreyabandhu
Pine Branch

Cézanne would have understood the problem
of a pine branch, its relation to the sky
in the early morning with just a sickle moon
and the sun not yet up among the rocks.

He would have felt its half-gesture – its arm
outstretched in something less than beckoning,
its pines cones open, flowering or shut.
He would have made it the subject of one of his

'experiments', felt with the tip of his brush
the branch's articulation – slender, more
slender – needles curling back, the thinnest
twig diamonding the blue or ramifying into it.

This

There's no law against my listening
to this thrush behind the barn,
the song so loud it echoes like a bell,
then it's further off beyond the lawn.
Whatever else there is, there's this as well.

There's no law against this singing –
nesting I suppose – up in the silver birch,
even though we build a common hell,
have done, and will make it worse.
Whatever else there is, there's this as well.

Philip Gross
from Something Like The Sea

All this way

by single rail track
through the forest,
by truck and by footslog,

by the last boat left
and leaving, by nights
in the open and years'

hiatus, *Nacht und Nebel*,
fog of someone else's
war. All this way

to arrive at an impasse
here, sixty years on, caught
in a sentence you can't finish,

your good neighbour
backing away, first nodding
then shaking his head

at unstoppable word-slur.
You're touching his arm
and he flinches

as if from the cling
of cobweb. All this way
to learn a life, to pass

through checkpoints, not to wear
the marks of silence on you
(like the names

not to be mentioned
in your censored letters home –
they'd leave their stain

on those you loved). All
this long way
to be a foreigner again.

Caroline Clark
What Is The Word –

What is the word for this
in French? The Russian I know –
a kind of chucking out. Brutal,
gets to the point though. The English
applies restraint. A thing mislaid,
mistake. A stately horsedrawn flourish.
Miscarriage, o, how ravishingly slow.

Dejan Bogojević
Salvador Dali

A piano set among rocks
and among cypresses

An illusion framed by the rocks
like a question
like a mute shadow
In the distance a little boat

The waves gleam white,
there are curlicues in the ether

'A girl by a window' –
her gaze burdened by a crumpled voice;
waterfalls in the morning light

The little boat in the distance...

The portrait ends

Michael Murphy
Turf

In my Calvin Klein pyjamas
And an ivory cashmere dressing gown
I am crashed out on our double bed.
Last night, I trimmed my beard
And clipped my fingernails, laying

The cuttings in the embers
Of yesterday's turf fire. This morning
When Felix opens the living-room
Door, a draught will wake the fire
And the white ashes glow.

I can smell the sweet turf.
We could be in Mayo, listening
To Michael and Pauline calling in
The milk herd to the yard
While overhead there's a noise

Of starlings on the telephone wires.
A lamb calls to its mother.
Between the fields the sky is growing
Light. There are no clouds. Not yet.
And then there are. And then

The flying shadows of the starlings skim
The whitewashed walls, and we see double.
But when the flock veers towards the sun
It is as though half the birds vanish
Into thin air. How strange to be alive

On a double bed in Liverpool,
While Felix brings me offerings
In the ash-coloured light.
He thinks I am asleep, and quietly
(He breathes as quietly as he can)

He ferries toys from his room
To this, and lays them on the altar
Of my chest. I must keep my eyes closed.
I guess by touch what it is he brings.
Later, I will peek while he is out of the room.

But not yet. Now I am in Mayo
And Eira will be helping Pauline
Feed the new-born calves a bottle.
The turf will be waiting in the shed
For me to fill a wicker creel

And carry it in to the living room.
The match is waiting in the box.
The flame is waiting in the match.
If only they were waiting for us, the days
We didn't use, the things we didn't mend.

Now Felix means to mend them
(A split indigo felt-tip pen, a three legged
Friesian cow – *Whisht!* – torn comics,
A hair slide that no longer grips,
Blue-tack that's lost its tackiness)

By building a pyre round his father –
Whose face isn't lost and drawn,
Whose hair isn't falling out
On the pillow, and who takes him
By the hand into a turf-dark shed in Mayo.

Ben Wilkinson
Open Return

Whatever brings us back to step off the second-to-last
train having shuttled down the West Coast mainline
here we go again: automatic doors open onto hail;
Victoria Park yawns; three or four pigeons dart
across laughing at those caught brolly-less in T-shirts.
A taxi pulls up. We clamber in, set off through silver-
streaked streets, half expecting to spot familiar faces
as the weather tunes down to sleet. But while the place
is the same, to us it's still changed – each landmark,
shop and side-alley pub a facsimile of its former self,
menaced by our memories of them; imaginings
no more real than streets in our driver's sat nav system.
On Queensway, a dog tied to railings looks on pitifully:
we pay, climb out and hurry on; my thoughts stuck with
that sail-less windmill which for years has sat redundant.
In the market square, the town hall's motionless clock.
Time flicking the Vs at us, having long since strutted off.

Daljit Nagra
The Thirteen O'Clock News

Pip Pip, today's feature for Monarchy Month is the first
Indian knighted, in 1842. His name is Sahib Jamsetjee
Jeejeebhoy. But why was a Queen keen to knight a native?

The answer lies with the man in a red 'phone-box',
the Arch Liberator, the Truth-Sleuth, you know him
as every lady's Tonk-Honker: Johhhn Simpsonian!!!

O John Simpsonian, do you Zoom Boom for us?
Pip Pip... our connection is scrambling... I'll be brief...
This self-made good chap had a chequered mid-life...

It seems that in Opium Wartime Jeejeebhoy ran
the speediest clippers bound for China... As you see,
I've landed at the port... at the Yangtze Gorge...

Those hordes of mango wood boxes are Jamsetjee's...
And the men with machetes are unloading each box
with brown balls inside as big as a comely lady's breast...

O John Simpsonian, through gyres and galaxies,
you're the boldest Zoom Boomer! *If I may sum up,*
in this dim droopy night... the love-sick mass of men

lined along the bank... as though a whole nation
of John Chinamen and Shangrilanders sleepwalking
for a toke, a cut, a suck of the dream of empire...

Omar Sabbagh
In The Beginning

I begin with this potted plant –
The bigger trees whose leaves dance
In the open-wide outside
Have different stories and
Different seers will tell them...

There's an empty chair standing before its
China blues and flowery reds, and
I don't know the names of the ghosts
Who come here to sit and inspect it, its rose
Colouring and rose scent.

I only know that it stands still, doesn't
Move or mummer in any way. And,
If I hang my watch on one of its leaves,
The time will be the same, I feel,
Hours later. It's captured here

As a spoken instance
Of an order of eternity
At a distance from us.
That's what I like about it:
That love's inside it.

Adam Thorpe
The Swimming Pool

Kinshasa, 1968

Our gardener would rake its gloom
like a patch of ground, stirring it

to a distressing, even darker core
of the almost-living and the nearly drowned:

scooped with a net for the rusty bucket,
he'd pour them out in the no-man's-land

before the proper bush: each night's haul
a sprawl of drunken guests, bristling

with sodden feelers and legs, still
in a rush to be free: capsized hulls with oars,

tiny nests of torment. Frogs swooped
between the slippery hair of the concrete sides

and the blind, sedimented depths
they'd jack-knife into. This was the door

out of the air's stickiness, the scratch of lawn:
our clumsy paradise. We'd swim with care

among the fresh spoil grown huge at eye-level
and so become forlorn: thorax still beating

and beating on a simple heart; mouth-parts
searching for air like a man's last words;

a moth's hopeless wingspread. Where
could I start? I handed out names to faces;

buried the drowned like birds.

WHERE IS THE NEW POLITICAL POETRY?
and
CENTREFOLD

Remember cities? Now the sky's
All that remains of them, the stars
Like broken glass.
                    – *Gwyneth Lewis*

John Burnside

Dear Hart Crane,

> We make our meek adjustments,
> Contented with such random consolations
> As the wind deposits
> In slithered and too ample pockets.

I'm sitting in a hotel room in Munich at five in the morning, sleepless, not unhappy and certainly not *depressed*, though maybe suspended, somewhat, between one state and another, the shadows gathered round, yes, but oddly neutral, so it feels like some kind of truce, some limited but adequate peace has been achieved between my ghost of a body and the night's slow unwinding. The hotel is next to the English Gardens and, through the open window, I hear its many and various birds, a wandering net of conversation and appeal that runs from the sugary maples and silver limes at this edge of the park to the awakening city beyond. I was out last night but I didn't drink, or not enough to make me sleep – though, for days now, the only sure path to sleep has been alcohol – and I am reminded once more that, for some of us, it's the better angels of our being who cause the most trouble, just as I understand, at the very back of my mind, that sleeplessness is a trouble worth having, a gift of sorts, to counteract the inattention of the daytime.

Now, I'm not one of those people who gets sentimental about company. I like being far from home and sitting quietly in a bare room listening to the dark. But this morning, for some reason, I think it would be good to go downstairs and find you in the lobby in your hat and coat, or sitting in the breakfast room, a rumba booming out from the house gramophone and you with your head down, pen in hand, blocking out everything so you can *write*. Blocking out everything; blocking out the world, while you sift random consolations from moonlight on a row of ash-cans or the fog of a harbour dawn leaning, for one last moment, on a cold window sill. I think it was the first poem I 'got', that *Chaplinesque* of yours, the one that begins "We make our meek adjustments...". And indeed we do. We don't want to and sometimes we're even brave about it, but more often than not there's compromise because, much of the time, 'the world' is too huge and too insistent on taking the least interesting path between two points. By which I mean, the moneyed world, the social order – whatever it has to be called, I'm not sure, that Authorised Version of vulgar rule where the goalposts are always in motion and the lies are so blatant it seems pointless to contest them. We make our meek adjustments… And there's nothing new in that, except that right now, in the second inglorious decade of a new century, we're so good at meek adjustment that we barely know we're doing it. The bankers rip us off with a brazen, almost experimental cynicism and, when the shit hits the fan, we blithely cut back on everything that is needful and good. The government pisses away our moral standing on far-off wars, fat cat landowners and corporations rake in astronomical subsidies from our taxes and fuel bills, self-proclaimed 'Greens' abandon the principles, if not the rhetoric, of social justice for the merest whiff of power-sharing (what does that *mean*?) – and we shake our heads, dismayed, but not surprised, our meek adjustments robotically clicking in, over and over again. Is it because there's so much consolation in art, so much beauty in ash cans and lonely, moonlit alleys, or have we just settled for consolations that, in some previous era, would have shamed us to the quick?

Oh, Hart Crane, Hart Crane... I loved you so much but then I tired of resignation and your dream of *a moment, now*, that is nothing more than the peace of the fathers and I got angry, to no real end. And I'm sorry, old friend, but I still think it's not enough: surely, there are better choices to be made and, as persuasive as your little tramp might be, it's time now for the spirit of Buster Keaton to rise up and lead us down the less travelled road – inventive, anarchic, potentially fatal – that you walked only for as long as you were able – wildly, desperately perhaps, and with the thick slide of the rumba somewhere in your bones as you sat alone, in a hotel lobby, scribbling verses on a beer mat or a lime-stained napkin, your face bright with dawn and attention and the notion, however fleeting, that a just rhythm could still make some difference in the world. It's almost enough, and it's not enough; because soon, maybe now, while the meek adjustments continue to be made, the epigraph you chose for *White Buildings*, a single line from Rimbaud, that most Keatonesque of poets, will rise, salty and razor-sharp on the wind: *Ce ne peut être que la fin du monde, en avançant.*

David Harsent

Three Poems For The World Wildlife Fund

Ocean

There'll come a day when doors open in the sea
and the drowned emerge to walk the salt lip of the shoreline.
On that day you might hear what seems to be

the fluting of wind on rock, though people say
there's music under the blue-green skim, music in the walls
of water, a slow percussion of drums and bells

in the wave-break; and the dead keep time as they go,
marking the beat with their footfalls,
their voices caught in the tug of the undertow...

They say: Look back from the last of the land
to the last of sky and sea, and know
this is all there is of it; this is all we have in hand.

These poems were commissioned to accompany photographs by Simon Harsent as part of the World Wildlife Fund/Leo Burnett campaign *Fragile Beauty*. The campaign itself took Silver for best photography campaign at the Australasian Writers and Art Directors Association Awards, and the individual images it was comprised of – Icefield, Ocean and Rainforest – each earned a Bronze for individual campaign photography. They won further prizes at the International Photography Awards, the Caxton Awards and at Adfest. The photographs and poems appeared as posters; the poems were also read on radio as part of the campaign.

The photographs can be seen on http://www.simonharsent.com

Rainforest

Between the forest floor and the canopy, a hothouse
that draws this shoot out of the delicate cast
of its pod: catching a blush of bruise as it lifts through the mash

of leaf and bone. Once in a hundred years…and the best
flower only in darkness: a plant so secret, so rare
that no one has seen it or named it or tasted its flesh.

Cure-all; elixir; hope against all hope…and this the last
of its kind. One press of the boot, one cut of the saw,
and who would know or care or count the cost?

Icefield

A place of ice over ice, of white over white
and beauty in absences. There was a time when the only sound
was the wind calling its ghosts, when the skyline was set

clean as a scar on glass, when your heartbeat slowed
with the cold, when your dreams brought in a white bird
on a white sky and music that could only be heard

from time to time on the other side of night.
Now the horizon's dark; now there's a terrible weight
in the air and a stain cut hard and deep in the permafrost.

Breakage and slippage; the rumble of some vast
machine cranking its pistons, of everything on the slide;
and the water rising fast, and the music lost.

I was very glad to be given the opportunity to collaborate with my son: first, because he's a first-rank photographer with an intriguing (often troubling) vision; secondly, because the WWF campaign provided a subject that concerns us both.

Many accept that the damage we have done – are doing – to the planet is now critical; a few do not. It's possible to see why those few might think as they do: it's difficult to give credence to a tragedy that is predicted but hasn't yet happened, just as it's difficult to be much affected by the human misery of war or natural disaster in a far country. The savage immediacy of such events stands at odds with a largely uneventful quotidian. Denial is an evidential response, but sensory rather than scientific. While life goes on as normal, the imagination has trouble stretching to a notion of the imminent chaos that climate change is said to promise.

In truth, the agencies of global warming are everywhere, though their effect is only visible to those in the front-line, where rain-forests are logged, where ice-fields daily diminish, where the seas thicken and clog. If the past is another country, so is the future: and a country not so far. The tragedy is there, waiting for our arrival.

John Kinsella

Paradise Lust: Damage Report

a subsection of Graphology

Fruits are sparse and there is no One,
unless overturner of stones and rocks
reveals itself: I have been searching,
keeping an eye out. In the penumbra
of valley last evening a pair of spinebills
protracting hill-curves, tonight,
a golden whistler semi-singing
glory. Distantly, noises
unsettling, disturbance.

The height of hills surprises;
there is no unitary voice;
the brook runs dry beneath its sand;

as provenance, kickstart day to kingdom come,
harrowed V enraptures gulches;
                              caprice,
a feast of bass and drum that booms
through woody cages:
                         petite histories
adding up, speech-positioned splendid
as eagle's wings, sizing, holding weight
of focus we're likely to myth-make,
our 'how it begins', or began, such
beginnings plastered across boards:
the *keep them out* ploy, environmental
furphy: no asylum here, we'll clear forests
but not the acre where *they* want to live.
Bigots have learnt the names
of animals they've helped make extinct:
now they utter them as talismans,
charms to ward off hijabs.

Is this how it begins?
                         Here, the mulga snakes
thickly swathe — we know they're here
and take precautions: I once hustled
one off the road by touching its tail;
                              joeys are out
of pouches, drinking beside their mothers
by the green waters
of farm dams.

            I've stripped names
away from censure: just rock and tree
and bend in the road. How will they claim
their readership? Make *take-away* outside specifics?
Greed and potlatch.

How many of Tim's little schoolmates have dads in jail?
Is jail the same as prison? a kid asks Tim. Yes.
Then jail is prison where Dad is.
Families keep sheep to keep the grass down.
Work the *Little Prince* equation.
Imbalance of stigmas.
I brag the politics of lock-up.

Developers and their 'horrid crews'
scout the district, following sales and making
estimates. I hand-write 'FUCK OFF' on the front gate
and brood:
          my handwriting so differs
from Tracy's, and she's generally more polite
(though not always). I locate bp nichol's *The martyrology*, Book 5:

'shapes the letters so unlike my own
infinite varieties of form & pressure
indexed by the measure chosen'

                       and reflect the register.
mixing of tone and timing to ease reception;
                       interlopers
(who owns what's 'settled' here?) *love*
saleability of light and colour: even drought-stricken
browns and yellow patch the blue dome to concert
standard:
          and the valley
resounds like an auditorium: hail, 'natural' acoustics.

'When we had a body in the 80s...'
                    Who said that?

Abolish 'summer' from your lexicon. Instil
the Time of Sulphur and Brimstone (requires
no vegetable matter). Paradise is perversely
abundant, concerting bushland to wonder,
medium-density housing, shops.

It's almost charity to nature.

What hides shepherd
view from loop
to see across
and measure
more from dead
tree exposure gleans
work of light
in God's enfolding: a certain percentage of cars
leave here taking people to houses of worship: gatherings
of group articulacy;

        we never thought of calling our son
Michael;

    never-ending torment of rivals
for life's disposability
serving entirety and enterprise,
gift for making hungers;

        such dated terminologies! text
of its time as radical as friends and colleagues,
eager readers wanting be: modern words burnt
by easterlies, swept inland by bleating
southerlies, bargaining granite and harsher rock,
making eye sockets of limestone,
residue of enthusiasm shaping images
of: nation
  self
  corporate façades
  family
  genus
  injury

     As when here the hills
shake with artillery
fire (the army bivouacs
40ks away, militarised wandoo forest

annexing ghostly protectorates, refuting
histories);
              it's told elsewhere if you're a believer,
making leaps and links and developing your conceits,
salvaging: ungracious voice
to work with here;

No wrath
No might
No exactitude
No stringing along, stringing out
No payback
No bargaining
No field to take or *nurture*;

                        quantify,
citizens! Quantify your living here with us,
on this block, alone to know how much we
don't and can't own: only its deletion, expiry,
scramble for title deeds that pre-exist
gloat and system: naturally, lashing. Naturally.

The 'bomb the boats' posse is brewing hate in
(inland) Northam. You see it
when you do your
shopping. Regional
centre where offspring of Displaced Persons
feed the zeitgeist. Place
of the Stolen Generations. Place
of removal and arrivals.
Fire of fear and fear of fire. Down pat.
Our daughter came home from school
traumatised, repeating racist diatribes,
and called perpetrators 'friends'. Accommodation, making do. Survival?
'Shame' has a local etymology, hi-jacked,
where does one begin?
Not in verse.

       Feeding on precedents, enslave
traditions, ends meet posturing anew
the new. Keep chiefly cock-a-hoop. Quest.

Adamantine seraphim, unholy war rollers,
wrecking ball riposte, full-length
blackened mulga snake, boombox
alcoholic valley-rage (crooning): what he means
is *live and let live*, unless you're a sheep
and he hates sheep unless he can eat 'em.

Vaughan Williams's trumpeter blows so much deadwood,
so many bases resprouted to die again, last chance
for roots to raise heads above the soil,
speak out against the sulphurous heat,
pathogens sweeping all aside;

                it's agony
watching this heaven so tainted, but the fall
is others' celebration: caveats on bushland count
for nothing, vacant spaces foraging vistas,
feeding 'seats of desolation'.

               Even so,
small song birds are *so* many and *so* confident
and flurry about my ankles like insects. Insects.
Really, who's to blame? That plume of smoke
last week from a 'controlled burn'
that had me riled and angry.
               Hot and windy day.
Patterns of flame sparkling in the volunteers' eyes,
goodwill and blind devotion a prayer to preservation
despite the risk. What gives?

We travel. We make comparisons.
Weigh up the options:

           Offenbach's *Orpheus*
in the Underworld replaces humidity

with gusto — I'd say 'raising its skirts',
but it doesn't work, and it's not me.
Though I can always character-play,
gainsay providence rousing chorus
following goddesses (literally) promenading
the gold town of Kalgoorlie, where water
is scarcer than gold: lexicon: cracks
in the street, Midas (mine) and Croesuses (mine)
and brothels on Hay Street (we slept soundly,
just behind), lead dust gold dust nickel
poetics up to Boulder names process
to refine lilt of light, desert's hemi-bloodiness,
pissed shiftworkers smoking Dawn at Norseman,
fly-in fly-out compensatory accommodation lack,
travellers experiencing telegraphs washed
beneath sand way way out, great woodlands
where shooting is off-duty labour of love and ennui,
to rave gung-ho brag source hauling earth
and racehorses glowing tracks, life-pay,
dry holes where Leviathan is rocked,
pilots flying small red flags to make
all you live in.

      Or deeper still, deep
east but close to bitten sea, borders dispensing
holographic Lilliputian islands, shelly
beaches, crabs and cuttlefish washed up
wrong-coded: leisure again: sea investments
and developers O developers scaly parasailing
rinds of boards and arch-evil's commercial breath: the depths
of narratives, interiors of an ocean we call Southern
though most others call Indian; all of them; (we)
arch-fiends are never singular, lolling
about in chains, thwarting barbecues,
making rhymes for beer and four-wheel
drives on the eternal beachfront, pleasures
of deteriorating poems: high winds, blast, vanquish.

Ian McMillan

Letter To The Man I Passed On The Street Today

Hello,

I don't know your name, but I've seen you before on my early morning walk; sometimes you nod to me but today your face is twisted in anger and you take no notice of me. I wonder why you're angry on this bright blue Monday. Have you missed your bus? Did the bus not turn up? Did you forget that the fare had gone up by ten pence and you didn't have enough money on you? Maybe you shouldn't have bought that Chunky KitKat at the paper shop, but of course in these tight times you need something sweet. So how about a poem? How about a nice Chunky Canto to soothe your day? I've got one here: it's one I've been working on since this ridiculous government of smooth-faced toffs took over nearly a year ago. It's a little portrait of my dad in his chair, not long before he died, casting his postal vote in a local election sometime around the turn of the century. His tongue is out and he's etching his cross on the ballot paper with a shaky hand. Outside Jackie-next-door is hanging washing out and there's somebody walking down the street. I guess, in my heavy-handed way, I'm trying to make the poem like Auden's 'Musée des Beaux Arts', and my dad is Icarus in a tie falling out of the sky and Jackie and the person walking down the street are the characters in the painting, in the poem, that notice nothing. The expensive delicate ship that had somewhere to get to. I know. A bit obvious.

Shall I read it to you? I've got it here. Or maybe I should encourage you to write one; maybe not now, I can see you're het up, but maybe we could meet later on at the library. The library's staying open, you know, at least for another year. I've joined the Friends of the Library. Let's meet there later on and you and I can write a poem together. (I know. This won't really happen. I would never walk up to somebody who was holding a Chunky Kit Kat in a threatening manner and suggest a one-on-one poetry seminar. But maybe I should. Maybe, in these terrible years, this is exactly what I should do.)

Wait a minute. I remember now: you're the person walking down the street in my poem, the one about my dad and the ballot paper. You're in a poem. You're in my poem. So why are you angry? What can poetry do to help? What can poetry do to change the world? Let's talk about it at the library. Quick, while it's still open.

Gwyneth Lewis

Letter To John Milton

Cardiff, April 2011

Dear Sir,

I met my English teacher from school last night at a book launch, and we talked about studying your masque, *Comus*, for A-level. Neither of us warmed to it – too much about chastity to make us really embrace the piece – but it occurs to me now that, in 1634, the masque must have been an equivalent of virtual reality today, and that the spectacle must have been a multimedia extravaganza, at the theatrical cutting edge. Mrs Osborne and I thought that we should probably have read the piece as science fiction and we would have loved it more.

You were my hero, though, once I'd read *Paradise Lost*. My wonder at the way you melded theology with politics and human psychology increased as I studied you at college, and did a special Milton paper for Finals. I was supervised by Geoffrey Hill, who made his students read you in seventeenth-century spelling and punctuation. I never did quite understand *Samson Agonistes*, but reading your political writings was a revelation. I'm still exhilarated by the passion of your rhetoric: "Give me the liberty to know, to utter, and to argue freely according to conscience, above all liberties." No one ever lobbied more eloquently for permissiveness combined with the moral discipline not to be deceived by facsimiles of the good.

I fear that you would be sadly disappointed in the quality of political debate today. You were Secretary of Foreign Tongues to the Council of State from 1649 but had been publishing pamphlets arguing for radical freedoms stemming from parliamentary democracy for a number of years before that. It's as if Alistair Campbell had written a philosophical defence of socialism, rather than managing the reputation of a particular politician, and then his own career as a celebrity.

This isn't to mention the way you traced the drama of democracy right back to first theological principles and to the fall of Satan, before Adam and Eve appeared in Eden. In this sense, the only figures comparable to you in modern letters are Stephanie Meyers, author of the *Twilight Saga*, and Philip Pullman who, you'll be pleased to know, has written a preface to a new edition of *Paradise Lost*. Meyers is a practising Mormon. While her heroine

Bella has been criticized by feminists for being too passive, I find the *Saga* as a whole to be a profound meditation on incarnation and its hazards as well as a moving love story. (I'm Team Jacob, by the way. If you don't know, it would take too long to explain.)

You're not fashionable at the moment and neither is the epic. The writer's writer of the seventeenth century is, rather, your erstwhile assistant, Andrew Marvell. I don't suppose that would trouble you. I saw on the television that your house is the most visited in the UK, which tells a different story. You would be interested in the way religion has become a contentious issue at the centre of intellectual debate. I'd like to see your arguments contra Dawkins and, equally, against advocates of Intelligent Design. As Marilynne Robinson (a Calvinistic novelist) has written, "Creationism is the best thing that could have happened to Darwinism." Your moral clarity on the pitfalls of loose thinking would be of great value to us now.

So, you're not forgotten. And if you could speak to us from the dead, I'd have one other question to ask, aside from guidance about contemporary attacks on religious faith, free speech and democracy. This one's personal: you were married three times and, though an advocate of divorce, you were widowed twice. How does the wife thing work in the afterlife? I'd love to know.

Hugs and kisses,
Gwyneth

From Our Sister's Bones

Gwyneth Lewis's new versions of the Clytemnestra story, two plays – *The Kill Floor* and *Our Sister's Bones* – are commissioned by Sherman Cymru and Clwyd Theatre Wales for production in spring 2012.

TIME   The future, when the food wars are being waged. Oil has nearly run out and the world has reverted to a tribal form of organization, there are armed struggles for food supplies. Technology is only patchily sustainable so society looks like that of a much earlier time.

SETTING   The Atreus family compound, the centre of a food business ruled by Agamemnon, who has been killed by his wife Clytemnestra. She's now running the business with her lover, Aegisthus. Times are noticeably harder

and leaner than in *The Kill Floor*. Iphigenia, her daughter murdered by
Agamemnon, has returned from the dead and the ghost of her father appears.

IPHIGENIA
Daddy, so sweet of you to come!

IPHIGENIA greets him like a hostess at a cocktail party. They air kiss.

AGAMEMNON
Oh, I wouldn't miss this for the world.
I'm avenged. That bitch, your mother, dead.
Her man… What happened to him? Not sure.
No matter. It can't be good. And you,
Sweet Geannie, running the show.

IPHIGENIA
Oh no, that's wrong. It isn't my show.
I'm merely… presenting so that they can see
How it unravels.

AGAMEMNON
                    So you're not a Fury?

IPHIGENIA
Au contraire. Are you?

AGAMEMNON
                              I am
A fury calmed. Appeased. Avenged.
The itch is scratched, the rash has healed.

IPHIGENIA
All right, all right! I get the idea.

AGAMEMNON
Funny how all that it requires
Is another body. Look at her there,
All bloody. I almost feel sorry…

IPHIGENIA
Hang on, I'm confused. You've been avenged,
So why are you here? Have you come to gloat?

AGAMEMNON
No, silly, though I have to say
It's a pleasing sight. When you die
Nobody tells you how hard it is
To stay in the grave if you've been murdered.

IPHIGENIA
You mean, blood spilt calls out to blood?

AGAMEMNON
And into language till that harries the living,
Drives them insane until something's done. Blah, blah…
Ad infinitum.

IPHIGENIA
                    But what about me? I don't hear anybody
Taking my part…

AGAMEMNON
                        Ah, you were a special case, my love.
You agreed to be killed, that makes all the difference.
You were a sacrifice.

*CLYTEMNESTRA'S FURY takes a microphone off a stand and prepares for a
solo in a spotlight.*

Oh, look, I think she's about to sing.
You know what she's like.This will be good,
Her voice is very strong, a deep contralto, like the castrati
They had in the harems…

IPHIGENIA
                    Who speaks for me?

AGAMEMNON
Your mother did that by killing me.

IPHIGENIA
I never asked her to! I never wanted it.
Do you believe me?

AGAMEMON
                              Course I do,
Sugar plum. Now hush, be quiet.

AGAMEMNON pulls IPHIGENIA to lean on his lap as he perches on a bar stool to hear CLYTEMNESTRA'S FURY sing. The mood of this song should resemble 'Hush Now, Don't Explain' sung by Billie Holiday.

CLYTEMNESTRA'S FURY
You did me wrong,
Don't matter now
Love goes on
Anyhow.

Look around you,
I'm behind,
Know you better
Than your own mind.

I'm your shadow
Wherever you go
The wrestling partner,
You'll never throw.

Stamp on me or
Blot me out
With light at noon,
I am the night

You did me wrong,
Don't matter now
Fear goes on and on
Anyhow.

Aviva Dautch

A Letter To Emily Dickinson

Tell all the Truth but tell it slant—

Your poem suggests "Truth" is like the sun – a dazzling thing when stared at straight on, "too bright for our infirm Delight". It seems to advocate the gradual, circuitous, explanation, the easing of truth, "Or every man be blind". Yet your language always reads as exactingly precise, so when you tell us "Success in Circuit lies", I can't help but believe you intend the double meaning of "lies": success may lie in circuitry, but successfully telling it slant may necessitate some falsification. Perhaps you're implying that creating artistic truth requires more than repeating literal truths? In *Proofs and Theories* (Carcanet, 1999), Louise Glück argues 'Against Sincerity', claiming "The artist's task, then, involves the transformation of the actual to the true." This postulates a gap between truth and actuality, suggesting that repeating actual truth in a poem is a reductive gesture – the writer's role should become that of alchemist, transforming or refining truth, using insight and aesthetics. I agree wholeheartedly with Glück about, well, almost everything in her essay. What makes me slightly uneasy is her phrasing – "the truth", "the true" – I'm uncomfortable with her use of the definite article for, on reflection, and after returning to your poem, I'm reluctant to admit there's such a thing as a singular truth.

Your choice of light as extended metaphor seems to depict truth as one authoritative, blinding, entity, but modern science has taught us that light is a spectrum of colour and nuance. Or maybe you knew that instinctively for, while your instruction to "tell it slant" is common currency today, less attention's been paid to the first part of your command: "Tell *all* the truth". One possibility is that you're refuting half-truths, fudges, misinformation and spin, but I'd suggest it's more than that – you're aware that "truth" is a prismatic concept. If so, it's a remarkable stance for someone with your Puritan heritage, although maybe we need to challenge the frequently superficial readings of your religious instincts. After all, Puritan belief in the doctrine of pre-destination includes what is said at the moment of death: calm acceptance indicating ascent to heaven. But you, who "heard a fly buzz when I died", have a less conventional response and should be placed in a more radical framework. And I'm Jewish, brought up in a Talmudic tradition of multiplicity and fragmentation where contradictory truths are allowed to co-exist: "these *and* these are the living words of God" (*Talmud Eruvin*: 13b) and the tension between is creative. Meaning is a "living" thing, constantly evolving and so always plural. The Rabbinic paradigm is to read every text on at least four levels: for the plain sense, the symbolic, the narrative and the mystical. Reading in this way makes me suspicious of Western linear thinking about a single religious truth or the epiphanic moment, and so despite, or perhaps because of, my religious upbringing, doubt is a constant presence. I know I share this with you; you wrote it down long before I thought it: "We both believe and disbelieve / A hundred times an hour, / Which keeps Believing nimble."

In *A Difficult Grace* (University of Georgia Press, 2000), Michael Ryan reminds us that poetry is your "vocation" not your "career", praising "how valuable for a writer keeping that distinction clear can be". It's great advice to a young poet, especially these days when so often we're advised to network as a way to get on, rather than to dedicate ourselves to craft. But even more necessary is what he continues to learn from you: "to see clear to the truth beyond oneself is still the poet's job and very great privilege". That seeing "beyond" is so important, and makes you, I think, a political poet. The word "political" has equally as wide a spectrum of connotations as "truth". A political poetics doesn't have to be polemical; in fact, and somewhat ironically, I'd argue it *mustn't* be polemical. For a polemical truth is a narrow truth – and it's our job to effect Glück's transformation and, even more than that, to enact an expansion of vision and understanding. A polemical poem is a closed poem, but your poems are open, offer their white space to the reader, make acute listening a necessity, and allow themselves to be illuminated by multiple slants of light. Thank you for them – they continue to astonish me with "Truth's superb surprise".

True Voice

for J.S.

Friday afternoon in Streatham. Sunlight
in winter, a weight of snow above us
on the glass conservatory roof. We should
have been cooking but instead we tuned in
the new LG TV with its *True Voice*
advanced technology. The channel didn't
matter, what we cared about was clarity
and pitch, the digital dialling down of
background noise, homing in on the frequency
of the newsreader's voice: far off famine,
wars, a politician sacked, another
celebrity whose phone was hacked. We sat
in the sweet spot, the speakers concentrating
sound, the timbre of the reporter's words
so resonant it could only be called prophetic.
This was what we'd paid for but even so
what pleased us – a quality of tone
richer than veracity – left me terrified.
All that evening, as we transformed secular time
into Shabbat, everything seemed heightened:
the candles, bread, wine, vibrating; each
molecule its own distinct, sacred, world.
The room oscillated with prayer, bouncing
off the glass walls until the snow shifted
over our heads, made the music of our
daily lives seem muffled: merely quiet
counterpoint to the defining Hebrew.
Was this epiphany? Or auto-tuning
our reality to one perfect note?
Looking upwards, I saw our blurred faces
reflected in a slipping surge of white,
attenuated as the background hum.

Ruth Padel

Wetbacks

for Issam Kourbaj

Mexicans cross a river, Cubans cross a fucking ocean!! Cubans are the
wetbacks, not Mexicans.
                    – www.urbandictionary.com

We're sitting on paint-splashed stools in your studio
sipping wine. You talk of Damascus, show me your design
for postboxes floating in air. How about those chairs, Issam?
"Ah Cuba! Ruth, the beach was dark with them. Full
of broken chairs! They tie them together and push off.
After seeing that I collected lost chairs from cellars,
skips, throw-outs from the restaurant downstairs,
to make a Migrant Monument in their honour."

From the sloping roof you unhook their legs. Oak, deal,
beech. All we need when chips are down: the shadows
of splintered wood. Like José Luis, forty-three, fridge repair-
man from Havana, who reached Isla Mujeres, Mexico,
in five days, riding inner tubes lashed to a weed strimmer
and piano lid, with a motor used for irrigating fields.

These two poems are taken Ruth Padel's forthcoming collection *The Mara
Crossing*, which addresses migration in cells, flora, fauna and human beings.

Ghost Ship

Off Ragged Point, Barbados, a six foot yacht adrift,
no name, no flag and a phantom crew. Eleven
young men still in bright shorts, orange, blue, red,
mummified in salt of their own sweat.
This is how we imagine we might go, when we wake
at night, afraid of moving on from Gambia
or Guinea Bissau. What you hear is redslick
in your temple. A ghost ship on Atlantic swell,
an airline ticket from Senegal, a note in a dead
boy's pocket, Excuse me, this is the end,
sorry to my family in Bassada, telling how
the skipper disappeared before they left Cape Verde.
How he could have jumped then, like his friend.
How they were towed, hawser slashed by a machete.

Jamie McKendrick

Letter To Pasolini

Caro Pasolini,

Some news about your play *Affabulazione*, which I've translated. The press responded with an intriguing mix of praise and blame: the blame mainly directed at the verse ("lofty lyricism", "florid", etc.) but there was also disgust at your chosen topic of a father's sexual obsession for his student son. Verse and incest are fine for the Greeks, you must have realized, but the moderns had better avoid them. The *Observer*'s critic entirely misconstrued one speech and accused you of "contradiction", a mistake copied by the *Guardian*'s critic in slightly more vehement terms. *Mah!* Grim as the play is, it was such fun to work on – your text, the great director and actors, the theatre – like having a life. So, *mille grazie*.

Reading your essays in *Passion and Ideology*, it crossed my mind that what we are missing is not so much politics in poems (though that may be its correlate) as a practice of criticism that has any claim to political passion. In an obituary Leonardo Sciascia called you a necessary gadfly to the culture. Our nearest equivalent is the poet and critic Tom Paulin. You share an acute aesthetic sense, a genius for unexpected connections and a rogue-Marxian formation. His anthology of *Vernacular Verse* and yours of dialect poetry is another convergence. Even the casual vituperation his work arouses is something you'll recognize from your own experience.

I have the impression that conflicts within the world of poetry in your time and place had some ideological substance. For us, the major divide would seem to be between *mainstream* and *avant-garde*, but the problem is that the *mainstream* isn't mainstream any more than the *avant-garde* is avant-garde. The quarrels are mainly illusory and stagnant. By temperament you might be drawn to the avant-garde camp, but would have little time for their assumption (deliberately ignoring history) that avant-garde poetics has some necessary connection with left-wing politics, and that the obverse holds: that traditional forms belong to the right. The philistine equation of politics and prosody, which you disposed of brilliantly in your defence of Umberto Saba's 'simple' forms and rhymes, is reiterated, as is the idea that clarity is commodified, ingratiating, populist and that complication is therefore complexity.

It's heartening that your ideological distance from writers such as Carlo Emilio Gadda and Giuseppe Ungaretti didn't impede your admiration for their work. On You-Tube, though, I found a fragment of your interview with Ezra Pound. I keep wondering if you knew the opening of *Canto XLI*, with his chummy reference to "the Boss", his regurgitated propaganda about the draining of the Marshes, and his gleeful hope that under Mussolini financiers (as "told by the mezzo-yitt") will be sent to the "*confino*". Hard to say which vice predominates – vanity, smugness, cruelty or servility – but the passage earns that insult Epicurus reserved for Plato and the Platonists: "Dionysiokolakes" – a tyrant's lickspittle. Your engagement with the desperate life of the Roman *borgate* is of an exactly opposite complexion.

Our own dispiriting conflict is also retrojected into the past. The avants lay claim to Eliot, Pound, Bunting, W.S.Graham, even Dylan Thomas, while the retros are dealt Kingsley Amis and Philip Hobsbaum. Talk of a stacked deck! Toilers in this field, like the late Andrew Crozier, Pierre Joris and now Robert Sheppard, insist that the mainstream is the Movement writ (not even) new. But the proliferation of lazy caricatures is common to both sides. If the air weren't so thick with phantasmal enmities, some of the actual differences might be explored. There's probably not much that would interest you in either camp, but who knows? – you read the poetry of your own contemporaries with such openness and curiosity.

Since your time, the internet should have made audible a host of other, unofficial perspectives – but instead, with some honourable exceptions, it's unleashed a rash of prejudice and pseudo-politics. Poets are judged according to their publisher, without the need to name or argue, or if they are named it's in the manner of "I've never read X but my wife says her work is execrable". I'll send you some links in case you have a celestial computer to hand, and want to while away some hours in this narrowest of *malbolge*. What a contrast your attack on Montale is. Your notion that he displays "a wounded, bourgeois sensibility" is too reductive, and you treat too many of his effects as formulae, though at least you argue through the evidence. But I think you were right to recoil from the vision of a contemporary poet being turned into a monument and, besides, you leave the reader in no doubt as to how good a poet you know he is. It's this kind of honesty that informs your passion – and the kind of thing, I'm afraid, the *Observer*'s critic would see as flawed by "contradiction". But yours is a mind that can make drama out of inner – as well as outer – conflict.

Cordiali saluti,
McKendrick

Omar Sabbagh

A Letter From A Poet To His Unconscious (aka: Mum And Dad)

In the artist of all kinds [...] one can detect an inherent dilemma, which belongs to the coexistence of two trends, the urgent need to communicate and the still more urgent need not to be found. This might account for the fact that we cannot conceive of an artist's coming to the end of the task that occupies his whole nature.

> – Donald Winnicott (q. in Adam Phillips, *Winnicott* (Penguin, 2007))

Dear Unconscious (or, Mum and Dad),
I am a battlefield. I am as much your battlefield as I am your progeny…

At different times in my life, to speak in terms of (personal) history, and as different aspects of the same moment in time, to speak synchronically, I have been the space where different and opposing tendencies have fought for domination: for a poet, experienced as fecund tension; as a human being, somewhat painful. The tension, deep in my unconscious, is I believe (on the evidence of what has repeatedly surfaced) between what Coleridge called 'fancy' and, following Kant, what he termed 'imagination'; between what Lacan called the 'imaginary' and the 'symbolic' registers; between the mother as loving container facilitating regressive delirium – a centrifugal force – and the effort of the father in me to make sense, give a sense of ending, interpret, anchor: a centripetal force. Both forces, the masculine and the feminine (not necessarily embodied in you, Dad and Mum), the positive and what resonates in the interstices of the ontic, are and have been integral to the process of poetic creation, the *mysterium tremendum* of creativity.

Without that feminine indulgence that causes the creative artist to regress and make use of regressive material, and that equally central effort of what Freud called 'condensation', no good or great art would ever be created. Which is to say that there is both an essentially subjective and an essentially objective moment in creativity. One's tone, attitude, music, persona come from what's deepest and most individual in one, and yet language is an alienation of the private self into an objective societal medium: what we share with others rather than that with which we differ. From T.E. Hulme onwards – especially for someone emerging fully-formed and later, like T.S. Eliot, these two forces have been termed the 'romantic' and the 'classical.'

The opposition works in another idiom as well. One might say that in so far as language is objective, that is to say, solely a medium to represent what is ontologically prior, it is classical. In so far (and I stress this as a major element of my own poetry) as the work of language is the very founding action of the existent – in so far, that is, as words are not mere media, but objects with material density in their own right – that particular sensibility Freud links with the schizoid – it is romantic.

And yet – both being elements essential to my poetry – which dominates?

Dialectically, it makes no sense to abstract away from the process of artistic creation. I would say that it is the very Oedipal tension of these two opposing forces, their visceral and vivid interaction, which is the poetic process, how it drives one in medias res. Another way of putting this is that, in order to represent, in however minor a way, poets, it's useful not to have obliterated one's Oedipal tensions by being (symbolically) castrated. The artist speaks most of and for the society embodied in him by being least tamed, least the common denominator of that same society. It is in this way that artists reach, expressively, what Lacan called the 'real', and what religious people may call God…

It is in the grind and tension of the two of you, as in the eternal repetition of a primal scene, that you both, Mum and Dad, bequeath me all my fertile pain, the heavy tricks of my artistry and the load of my artistic destiny. Thank you, and I love you.

George Szirtes photo: Clarissa Upchurch

Sarah Wardle

11th April, 2011

Dear Family,

Anniversaries are a time to take stock. This Easter it will be twenty years since I left Oxford in a whirlwind of mental ill health, having thought I was Jesus in order to explain both the extraordinary calm that had come over me and the fearful sense that I was being targeted to be killed. This was all the more odd because I have always been an atheist, but they say that *in extremis* those who have faith lose it, while those who do not, believe. I wrote about these thoughts and feelings in my first book, *Fields Away*, in poems such as 'Cosmic Confusion' and 'Rhapsody in B Flat': "Christ, take flight".

Like many writers who are susceptible to bipolar illness, since the spring of 1991 I have been forced, through periods of mental ill health, to sample psychiatric inpatient care, and I can say that it is the poor relation of the Health Service. Governments on both sides of the political divide clearly think that here is a group of people whose vote they can afford to lose, who by virtue of disability cannot mobilise themselves to be heard. Lack of purposive activities and access to fresh air and an outdoor area, understaffing and bullying, are rife on mental health wards. When patients argue and try to leave, the rapid tranquillisation that follows causes smirks of pleasure on the faces of some of the nurses involved in the procedure: some get a kick out of knocking a person when they are already down. Other young women, as well as myself, say of R.T. that they thought they were going to be raped. I expressed this belief in poems in *Fields Away* such as 'Flight', and detailed a year spent as a psychiatric inpatient in my third collection, in which I aimed to make *A Knowable World* of the helplessness and panic involved in bipolar disorder.

I have witnessed some "care"-users make bids for suicide and succeed, whether accidentally or intentionally I shall never know, though I have no doubt that the system drove them to their deaths. These young women – and I describe one in 'For Michelle Farrell': "The ward is still filled with your Irish spirit, / like the time you called the doctor a 'Fuckwit'" – get pushed under the rug by Coroners' Reports, which attribute their deaths to long-term addiction, or describe a jump from a building as a characteristically "impulsive act of self-harm". On one occasion nurses were sacked, but management and psychiatrist jobs stay intact – although a young psychiatrist who worked in the intensive care unit of a hospital I have written about committed suicide himself.

While I faced adversity both from within, in the form of misfiring synapses, and from an environment in which other patients kicked off while the television blared all day (I now do not possess one), family provided a steady stream of visitors. On one occasion, when I was resisting medication because of its association with force, Grandmother brought me the gift of a bottle of perfume called 'Poison' to brace me up! Family, with your unflinching support and care, which has helped me overcome my fear of medication – not least because you, Mother, are now a year clear of cancer with the help of medical treatment – I can lead a normal life.

But for many trapped in the system this is not so, and I pay tribute to them in 'Hotel Gordon': "all these I mean, people lost in the in between / of life, as some make good and others fall back". Father, I voted for you once I was old enough, and since you left Parliament have voted left-of-centre, but successive governments have failed mental health patients, and politicians on both sides must address this iniquity. With more Government cuts looming, I fear for inpatients, who deserve a better standard of care, tolerance and understanding, and for those who receive treatment in the community but who are not sustained by the unstinting personal support you have given. An underfunded mental health service means many whose families have washed their hands of them get little care: meanwhile, the determination in the face of bewilderment, the pain and the sacrifice of families like you, who keep on caring, helps those like me to pull through. Thank you.

In hospital I wrote about you both in 'After Ralph Vaughan Williams', and I would like to end on that note:

> *The Lark Ascending* is my parents' lives,
> running the currents of the skies,
> buffeted by each downward blow,
> riding the eddies of air below,
>
> as if each upturn and turbulence
> is caused by me and is my fault,
> but the music's pity is that the flight
> ends in their spirit rising out of sight.

With all my love –

Sarah Maguire

I founded the Poetry Translation Centre in 2004 (thanks to the Arts Council's generosity) with two aims: to ginger up poetry in English through translating contemporary poetry from Africa, Asia and Latin America; and in an attempt to engage with the countless thousands of people now settled here for whom poetry is the highest art form, as it is for anyone from an Islamic background. The many Somalis, Sudanese, Pakistanis, Kurds, Afghans and Iraqis living here are equally fervent in their devotion to poets and poetry. So what better way to make them feel welcome than to translate their most highly esteemed poets into English, using the skills of talented linguists working with closely leading British poets (such as Jo Shapcott, Sean O'Brien, Lavinia Greenlaw and W.N. Herbert), with the additional hope that these brilliant translations might engage English-speaking audiences too? And that meetings between these remarkable international and local poets might change their writing and, perhaps, their lives?

Mohan Rana (India)
The Cartographer

Between the lines it's you,
absent, but a silent presence
just as the rain is absent in the passing clouds.
There you are, absent, in every empty space
of life. In every gap of time
on these panic-stricken roads.
I don't look out any window,
I don't stop at any door
I don't watch the clock
I hear no-one's call.
As geography changes its borders,
fear is my sole companion.

Translated from Hindi by Bernard O'Donoghue and Lucy Rosenstein

Reza Mohammadi (Afghanistan)
Spring

Spring came and put on your shoes
Spring came and took you on a journey
Spring came when you were sleeping
and made her bed by your side

While you slept
she infused you with her spirit
and dyed you with fresh blood

Spring gave you a new name
and bought your freedom

Clouds blessed your home
and called your name

Stars burn *shisha* in your room
Your mood, your breath, your heart
take flight like a bird

The wind sweeps through your bedroom
You dress yourself with the morning breeze

Now you and spring are one
Spring gave you a new name
So love came and put on your shoes

Translated from Dari by Moheb Mudessir and The Poetry Translation Centre Workshop

Euphrase Kezilahabi (Tanzania)
Floods

I will write a song on the wings of a fly –
Let this song make music when the fly flies, let everyone hear it.
The poetry of rubbish will be sung
on the wounds of farmers
and on the pus they sweat.
I will write on the wings of insects
and everything that flies,
on the zebra's stripes
and the elephant's ears,
on the walls of toilets, offices and classrooms,
on the roofs of houses, the walls of the government,
and on scarves and t-shirts.
This is the song I will write:
This year's floods threaten old houses in the valley;
people have begun to leave;
electric cables have been destroyed –
where there once was light, now it's dark.
The floods this year!
And old tree has fallen down next to
our rickety houses.
We don't sleep when the fierce wind blows.
Everyday we examine its roots
the rickety walls of the house,
and the branches that must be severed from its trunk.
The floods this year are a warning...
We shall tell our grandchildren:
The floods that year
many trees were felled.
The floods this year
many of us will perish.

Translated from Swahili by Katriina Ranne and The Poetry Translation Centre Workshop

Ian Duhig

Will There Also Be Singing..?

It seems to me that the biggest change in UK political poetry is not the commonly-mooted notion that the younger generation of poets are uninterested in politics, but one that flows directly from the much greater involvement (resembling more the US situation) of all poets with academia, whether as fully-fledged academics or in the semi-detached positions which I have enjoyed in the past. Although Town-and-Gown divisions have always existed here, universities are even less local institutions than they used to be. As Slavoj Žižek's *In Defence of Lost Causes* puts it, "a New York academic has more in common with a Slovene academic than with blacks in Harlem half a mile from his campus" which, *mutatis mutandis,* would also be true of where I have lived in the UK, and of Ireland. This process parallels larger patterns of globalisation where, in Terry Eagleton's blunt words from *After Theory,* "the rich have mobility while the poor have locality". Locality's presence in poetry has almost become an index not of economic poverty, but of ambition and talent. Yet a confusion of Seamus Heaney's distinction (discussing Kavanagh) between parochialism and provincialism is common now – someone wrote not long ago that he would be happy to be described as any kind of poet, except a local poet. ...Not even a John Clare, who panicked at being "out of my knowledge" when he walked too far from his village?

Inevitably, academic political poetry will be very different from local politically-informed poetry. Once, in an interview, I was asked why I employed traditional forms when writing about homeless people; naively I answered that I felt it lent my subjects' stories more dignity. However, I haven't come up with a better way of expressing this since, so it will still have to do. Obviously, this sort of thing isn't terribly relevant to debates about traditional forms that take place in universities. But my concern here is to note that these debates take a different direction outside universities, and that outside universities poets still survive to have these debates at all.

The most recent campaign with local political dimensions I have been involved with was the David Oluwale Memorial Appeal. This really got going following the 2008 publication of Kester Aspden's *The Hounding of David Oluwale,* which made previously-classified information on the case available for the first time. Somehow, for many people Oluwale's fate embodied a world of wrong, in a way that recalls the words of the Qur'an: "If anyone kills a person... it is as if he kills all mankind". Oluwale's case had made a big impact on me, as the first local job I had in Leeds after moving up from London was in Hepworth's cloth warehouse, where Ken Kitching, one of Oluwale's police tormentors, was employed as a security guard (having just been released from the short time he served in prison). My workmates told me the whole dirty story, which I won't repeat – it's easily found on the web. It fed into many influences which led me to spend most of my working life in the field of homelessness.

There was a strong non-academic cultural presence in this campaign: the BNP/EDL code for immigrants as "cultural enrichers" perhaps meant that we felt it incumbent on us to prove the truth beyond their sneer. Corinne Silva's film *Wandering Abroad* was given a run in the City Art Gallery. Caryl Phillips wrote about Oluwale in in his book *Foreigners*. Dipo Agboluaje's play based on Aspden's book, and with the same title, toured nationally. Was the campaign successful? Yes; an area close to where David Oluwale drowned was proposed by the City Architect for "some form of memorial garden or terrace", though negotiations are ongoing. And the campaign may have been symptomatic of, or contributed to, changing local attitudes in a period when Leeds lost its sole BNP councillor, returning a new Labour administration to the City after a deal with the Greens and countering a regional trend which returned a BNP Member for the European Parliament.

The cliché is that race, not class, is the real social issue in the US, while the reverse is true here. In fact both are urgent in both places, now class means one of the walls of social inequality. But here, questions of race are resolving into mealy-mouthed Multiculturalism-versus-Midsomerism discussions. To me, immigration as locally experienced has clear national and international significance, after the success of Marine le Pen in France, and with similar parties to her National Front rising all over Europe and Scandinavia. Although some reading this may wonder what local issues like the Oluwale campaign have to do with them in their more "civilized" parts of society, this country, or the world, I would ask them to think again. There is a tendency now to devolve unpleasant things – cuts and poverty by the Coalition, or responsibility for shameful attitudes by enlightened societies at large – to the fringes of a society or nation. Meanwhile the local view here would devolve responsibility for the dead of Iraq and Afghanistan onto New Labour, and that party's desperation to ingratiate itself with a wealthy South-east and the USA. North American poets and commentators on poetry frequently express impatience with the class and regional issues that complicate this small island's lives, but the North/South divide here is becoming more, not less marked. We are developing a modern version of what Procopius described:

> In Britain, men of ancient times built a long wall cutting off a large part of it [...] to the south of the wall there is a salubrious air, changing with the seasons, moderately warm in summer and cool in winter. But on the north side, all is reversed in a home to countless serpents and wild beasts [...] Natives believe any man crossing this wall will be struck dead immediately.

Well, if not struck dead in body, in danger of boring stiff those they talk to about it.

Unlike Clare, being "out of my knowledge" is a condition I experience most of the time, so my prediction in the last paragraph needs to be taken with a bushel of salt. I never imagined that the social inequalities that were being swept away in my youth would return and become even more entrenched now. I would not have believed that the council estate I grew up on would be sold off despite increasing need. I left school at sixteen, but found my way into higher education through night-school free, and easily; yet I did not develop the mental faculties to foresee that my son's generation would be saddled with decades of debt for a less valuable qualification. My wife and son both work for the NHS... but you get the idea. If poetry begins in wonder, such stupefying political changes could not fail to influence mine, as they do many other poets now, writing in many different ways. I'll end with Brecht, doing our job in a considerably worse situation:

> In the dark times
> Will there also be singing in the dark times?
> Yes, there will also be singing
> About the dark times.

from Skew Bridge Sonnets

I. Wrong Turn

> *Later, the language of the people, which up to then had been known as*
> *Trojan or Crooked Greek, was called British.*
> — Geoffrey of Monmouth, *The History of the Kings of Britain*

Askew from Skewsby, but not too far,
and just a digression from Shandy Hall
though harder to find than Shangri-La,
they built a new Troy without any walls
or signposts (to baffle Greek invaders);
remaining unmarked on motoring maps,
this smallest of all Britain's turf mazes
was never designed as a tourist trap,
but turns like a sonnet to trap Old Nick –
as he can only move in a straight line,
the locals say, who might seem thick,
still shy of strangers and their designs,
but if in the end they choose to speak,
it sounds like Trojan, or Crooked Greek.

II. Doubling Back

Our language can be seen as an old city: a maze of little streets
and squares... In the actual use of expressions we make detours.
　　　　— Wittgenstein, *Philosophical Investigations*

Strangers ask, *Why the 'City of Troy'*?
The answer to this turned into a maze –
it's lost in translation; a turn of phrase
unwinding from the old Welsh *Caerdroia*,
where *Droia* was 'Troy' but 'Turns' as well...
so runs the web's unByzantine explanation,
But does *Caer* mean 'City'? Isn't it 'Castle',
as in Caernarfon, whose Byzantine walls,
like Byzantium itself, are also translations,
Roman to Greek – yet still Greek in Wales
as its conqueror's words to local Britons
who he made slaves, working like Trojans,
now called 'Welsh', "English" for 'Strangers'
(from invaders' *extraneus* and *étrangers*)?

III. Skew Bridge

I felt quite at home, / As if it were mine, / Sleeping lazily / In this house of
fresh air.
　　　　— Sora, in Bashō's *The Narrow Road to the Deep North*

I knew I was lost passing the Ross Maze Museum
a third time, late for connections at Skew Bridge.
Missing the Orient Express, the Troy quinquireme,
the last magic carpet and Pharoah's golden barge,
I settled with ghosts from its old navvies' shanty
to drink in that night the spirit of the navigator,
whose camp might mean a song, or build upon *tŷ*,
the Welsh word for house, our house of fresh air.
I turned in and dreamed of a nearby skew bridge,
built yearly from fresh words which only connect,
though turning like pages, a verse-end or sonnet,
or any of the coats worn by the English language.
I slept soundly. When I woke and rose next day,
I found a thousand years had passed away.

Knut Ødegård

The Honorable writer Knut Hamsun
The tomb in the garden
Nørholmen
Grimstad

Maestro Hamsun!
I'm writing to you in your disintegrated state, there below the soil you loved more than anything, maybe with the exception of the passionate eroticism whinnying like wild stallions through the pages of your books. We both believe in the existence of the spirit beyond the corruption of the flesh, and therefore I take the liberty of approaching your immortal soul. Dust is dust, spirit is spirit. But how stand matters in regard to your soul?

I know you've heard this before: How could you, writer of profound internal issues of spirit and charity (oh yes: *Victoria*), defender of the rights of the soil: how could you give your affection to the demons? The white skull with the finely arced forehead smiles its unfathomable grin below ground. But I wonder how you could be so clear-sighted in matters of the future, and simultaneously so blind to your own time?

Two images bother me. One is to be found in *Mysteries* when Nagel, the enigmatic stranger, enters the small town carrying a violin case. He books a room at the hotel, where the maid stealthily opens the lid of the case to view the instrument. But alas, there is no violin, but dirty clothing, scraps of paper, writing gear. The other image is of you, Maestro, when on May 17th 1943 you sit down at Nørholmen and write to Joseph Goebbels, "Nobel inaugurated his prize for last year's idealistic writing. I don't know anyone who so unselfishly year after year has written and spoken on the matters of Europe and humanity at large as idealistically as you Mr. Reichminister. I humbly ask you to excuse me for sending you my medal."

Back to the first image. What seems curious is not Nagel's violin case packed with dirty laundry, but that he *is* actually able to play when an instrument is put in his hand: "His sudden appearance outside the planned programme and in the middle of the auditorium where it was fairly dark, his strange countenance, the wild dexterity of his fingers that confused everyone and gave them a sorcerer to behold". The audience is mesmerized. But then, "after four or five minutes he drew the bow across the strings in the most frightful manner, a desperate howl, a sound so impossible, so upsetting that no one any longer knew what was going to happen, three four strokes with his bow like that, and then he suddenly stopped." This screeching discord is what we hear when you write to Goebbels, and in that instance it may be explained as the human weakness of opportunism. But the real howl of desperation is what we hear on May 7th 1945, when the Norwegian *Aftenposten* prints your obituary to Adolf Hitler. You write that he was "a warrior for humanity and an evangelist of the gospel proclaiming the right of all nations."

You knew it was all over, Maestro, and yet you still...

The great puzzle is that in your writing you saw more clearly than others how the international market economy would enslave people a generation later. Equally clearly you foresaw the need, when everything had turned into industry and everyone moved to the big cities, to protect Mother Earth. That after all people live on the fish in the sea and the "Crop of the land". This was the crux of your simple message. Yes, how could *you*, in particular...? Nagel's answer is: "Well, one has to astonish the world you know, without shyness..." And, when asked about his final discord: "I wanted to step on a demon's tail". Maybe you, Maestro, stepped on the tail of contemporary demons, playing with the powers of evil without ever confronting the demon's spirit? Is the answer that you were an aesthete; that the magic of spectacle, the show of the despicable spirit of the time, interested you? You cherish Nagel, he who could astonish the world, and show no interest in what he was beyond that magic. You show us your heroes, the invincible ones, the ones who bewitch spectators or force the soil under their plough. But the weak, you say somewhere, are that soil's fertilizer.

So is it the soul and not the spirit that is your concern, all the way from beginning to tragic end? The soul bound by soil, blood and clan? Is it in this image that we see the whole predicament of your project? That industry and a market economy were simply a threat against blood and soil? Is there after all a deep and dark connection between your seducer Abel and your farmer Isak?

I guess I can't expect an answer from the cemetery soil. The skull, quiet and still with its grin, the fragile bone pipes, are without sound. No wind down there, only the imperceptible movements of the centuries in those depths.

Your devoted admirer,
Knut Ødegård
Hol Gård, Molde

Maureen Duffy

All I ask is the privilege for my masculine part, the poet in me (if any such you will allow me) to tread in those successful paths my predecessors have so long thriv'd in, to take those measures that both the ancient and modern writers have set me, and by which they have pleased the world so well. If I must not, because of my sex, have this freedom, but that you will usurp all to yourselves: I lay down my quill and you shall hear no more of me.
— Aphra Behn, Preface to *The Lucky Chance*, 1686

To Madam Behn at her lodging in New Street:

My dear,
In your last you required to know how we women poets did now that we have a woman laureate, who is treated with that honour you were denied although satirized in your time as The Female Laureate. Though there are now many more women poets than in your day (as there are many more citizens even of London and the world), and some of 'em acknowledged to be of the first rank, which only Katherine Phillips, the Matchless Orinda, was among you (apart from among your own friends who wrote their praises of you into the many commendatory verses to your several collections) yet we have not progressed against the more subtle forms of discrimination as you would expect.

You boldly spoke out in your own defence and in defence of women to have the full freedom to write on any subject and in any terms, rejecting any suggestion that there was anything in the masculine makeup, apart from their better education, that made them better equipped to be poets, and even that, you said, was not necessary to being a good writer. Yet if one of us was to speak out in such terms we would be sneered at as 'feminist', as if that was itself a mistake, and dubbed by some 'hysterical dykes'. We are told that we have enough equality yet you have only to count up the number of male and female writers reviewed in the literary pages. So too, although a woman has won the most prestigious fiction prize, that form that may be said to have been first successfully written here by you, (although Defoe is still accorded that honour), nevertheless women's fiction is still not given the serious and equal attention that it should have, and the Orange Prize, Virago and Only Women Press remain necessary to attempt to redress the balance.

As for the canon of English poetry it is still a largely masculine preserve, and your own talents largely unappreciated tho' I must confess the literary achievements of your age are woefully under-represented even in the theatre where they were so manifest. You will remember that your admirer, Virginia Woolf, said that we women should all lay flowers on your grave, while demanding true equality and a room of one's own, which I take to mean the freedom and the means to write, and be free of that stereotyping which would channel us into the domestic and the sentimental away from politics and 'ideas', as well as sex, all of which you tackled in your day.

There will be some who will regard this as a trivial issue yet it is but the outer fringe, the shallows as it were, of more dangerous discriminations which stretch from the so-called glass ceiling for women in board rooms or the cabinet, even in the way parliament conducts its business like a bear garden where women's voices are easily drowned out, through domestic violence, forced marriage, honour killings, female circumcision and numerous such horrors unknown among the Caribs when you visited them. Low level discrimination in all areas still masks our hidden inequalities so I have brought these matters to your attention knowing how bravely you spoke against those which might have caused you to lay down your pen in disgust, and that we should continue to salute you for it, and for your presentation to the world of your noble black slave, Oroonoko, and his struggle for freedom.

I remain, madam, your devoted follower in the demand for true equality in every sphere of life.

Neil Rollinson

Dear Bysshe,

I'm not often given to writing letters to my poetry heroes, especially ones as eminent as yourself, an early poetic role-model and a presiding spirit of the poetic imagination. But we're living in cynical and selfish times, and I thought I'd let you know how things were here, at the moment. I wonder what you'd make of it all. I reckon that, as the standard bearer for a poetry of dignity and political conscience – the long fight against authoritarianism, despotism, bigotry, patronage – and a champion for all that is fair and right, not to mention a believer in the power of poetry to move and change things, you'd be amazed at the state of the poetry world right now, how stagnant it is, how bogged down in petty infighting and back biting, how mired in sloth and inaction, how solipsistic and self important it has become.

It's not as if there aren't any causes. The same ones you fought for and wrote about are still in evidence nearly two hundred years later, you'd be amazed by that no doubt, but poetry has gone soft. It no longer engages with these issues. We are at war in at least two countries, inequality is rife at home, there is poverty and deprivation up and down the country, but our poets seem more concerned with feathering their own nests and preparing for some kind of posterity. The torch of protest is being carried now by songwriters, playwrights and film-makers, without a whimper from the poets. It is rare indeed these days for poetry to shock or challenge the status quo, the safe and comfortable middle-class *laissez faire*, although a few names come to mind: Harrison, Reading, Zephaniah, O'Brien, poets whose work I think you would most definitely approve. But the names are few.

Reading your *Mask of Anarchy*, a poem that is rightly feted now even though no one dared publish it for twenty years after the Peterloo massacre, one feels astonished at its power; its impudent, damning and incisive argument. Would you have written that second brilliant and chilling stanza about our own recent Prime Minister Tony Blair, whom many people see as war criminal?

> I met Murder on the way—
> He had a mask like Castlereagh—
> Very smooth he looked, yet grim;
> Seven blood-hounds followed him:

Of course your good friend Byron wrote, on the death of the then Leader of the Commons:

> Posterity will ne'er survey
> A nobler grave than this,
> Here lie the bones of Castlereagh:
> Stop, traveller, and piss.

It seems inconceivable that a major poet would write verse like this today; and certainly not directly about a political leader.

You might think that while the big issues are perhaps intimidating, poets could get their teeth into *politics* with a small *p*, and write challengingly about the personal sphere, human relations, sex and the domestic landscape. These issues are still often a battleground, and rife with conflict and inequality. Poets could be writing with generosity in these areas. But again the names are thin on the ground: Alvi, Kay, Shuttle. Daffodils are the order of the day.

We have the Laureateship, yes, even now. Nothing much has changed since the days of Southey and Wordsworth it seems. Even worse than torpor and lassitude is the fashion among poets for taking royal and political patronage, something that would surely turn your stomach. There are more officers of the Order of the British Empire with pens in their pockets than you'd care to imagine. Excuses abound of course: I took it for my Gran, for the hard working people behind the scenes, for the poetry world in general. But take it they did, though there are exceptions: Zephaniah and Shapcott among them. For me this is worse than appeasement. When the Establishment have signed up the last poet, who will be left to stand up for socialist/left-wing values, or indeed just plain human rights, those values you and other Romantic poets sweated blood for? Who would have thought that genuflection would ever be synonymous with poetry?

You might not believe it, but if you were writing now you would still manage to scandalise contemporary social mores. Poetry no longer seeks to challenge the social order, or the political establishment: on the contrary it seem to want to roll over and have its belly tickled, or worse, it wants to become part of the very thing it used to despise, that it always fought against so proudly. Yet we all remember your immortal phrase in *A Defence of Poetry*: "poets are the unacknowledged legislators of the world".

CENTREFOLD

Night By Night: David Harsent

SEAN O'BRIEN

It is often the case that when we try to focus on a literary grouping its apparent members begin to escape definition, proving themselves exceptions to a rule which quickly ceases to be applicable or useful. The Movement is a well-known recent example. At this distance it certainly looks like a series of occasions and broad affinities rather than a movement: anything resembling a manifesto was administrative rather than revolutionary, and not for the last time the real value of the name of a literary tendency was to give its opponents something to aim at, as in Charles Tomlinson's famous essay 'The Middlebrow Muse'.

The poets associated with the magazine *The Review* (the severity and scepticism of which might be taken as a kind of manifesto) and in some cases with its successor *The New Review*, both titles edited by Ian Hamilton, never gained or sought the kind of collective publicity accorded to the Movement, although Clive James guyed some of them as Hugo Harsfried – Hugo Williams, David Harsent and Michael Fried, a list to which can be added the putative leader, Ian Hamilton, plus Dunn and Colin Falck and, occasionally, John Fuller. The conviction behind *The Review* seems to have been that poetry was extremely difficult to write, never mind write well, and that most people should be ruthlessly discouraged from attempting it.

This was certainly the line taken in Hamilton's trenchant book of essays and reviews, *A Poetry Chronicle*, although his anthology edited with Falck, *Poems Since 1900* (1975), which now seems largely forgotten, was marked by brevity and relative conservatism and what might have seemed an unexpected enthusiasm for A.E. Housman – until the romantic pessimism of several of the *Review* poets, Hamilton is particular, is taken into account. The anthology also includes a very funny poem, 'History of a Literary Movement', by Howard Nemerov – himself no avant-gardist – in which the leader begins to doubt the relevance of Impli, his last remaining acolyte.

Apart from gender, what momentarily linked the very different poets associated with *The Review* was an interest in brief, often minimalist dramatic lyrics – poems without scaffolding or exposition. David Harsent's early work, *A Violent Country* (1969) and *After Dark* (1973), has a greater range than Hamilton's main collection, *The Visit* (1970), which deals with painful, obliquely rendered occasions of love and loss. Harsent is a love poet too, but he also deals with myth ('Legendry'), history ('Old Photographs') and, most interestingly, he offers a powerfully aestheticized appreciation of the world when nothing is happening, in 'Cockade'.

All these poems show Harsent working towards the approach which comes to characterize his idiosyncratic version of dramatic lyric, in which lyric impulse and musical shape are used to substantiate a narrative context from which important elements are often withheld. The effect is sometimes akin to watching a film in a foreign language. The climate is one of ritual and obsession, with the lives of animals – hares, greyhounds, hawks – taking place in emblematic parallel. The extended 'Dreams of the Dead' (1977) draws the reader in, again without explanation, to read things in the terms set by the narrating voice, often apparently in the no man's land between dream and waking reverie. It is no surprise that Harsent has been in demand as a librettist, given his ability to offer emotional substance in minimal form.

His world at this stage has people but no society: even the outdoor world seems sealed in privacy. Harsent's sharply, sensually rendered, usually rural landscapes are the sites of eroticism and violence, with hints of war in the background, and a sense of perpetual crisis and withheld revelation. The section titled 'July 3' combines most of the main motifs, opening with the group of (we infer) Edwardian women in a typical setting: "The sweep of their skirts leaves tracks in the morning wet. // One whistling a tune, and one / hanging back from the rest / to watch a poppy's petals smudge to mauve / as they are torn [...]". This is rather like reading Kipling's 'The Way Through the Woods' rewritten on the other side of modernism and with a pervasive eroticism brought to the fore: "Their high-necked blouses dampen, / a pool / of moisture at the hollow of the throat; / the cling of cotton at their calves and thighs." Unlike Kipling's, Harsent's mystery offers no comfortable repose. At first sight these lines recall the glowing Julie Christie in Joseph Losey's film of *The Go-Between*, but while the narrator of L.P. Hartley's novel begins by saying, "The past is a foreign country; they do things differently there", Harsent's poems add the implied rider that we shall never discover precisely what it is that they are doing so differently, and that the imagination is charged and goaded by this dramatic uncertainty. Looking for assurances in this world to whose inhabitants we have not been properly introduced, readers learn to rely on Harsent's unfailing ear for the underlying iambic shape of his lines.

Mr Punch (1984) is a grimmer piece of work: "Quicklime in the pit, that's more his style." Among others things the book dramatizes aspects of male sexuality and psychopathology. "These women are all alike to Mr Punch. // He'd like to own them, he'd like to eat them whole, / he'd like their murders / feeding his night-time conscience." In all, *Mr Punch* can be read as a riposte to the inflation and excess of Ted Hughes's *Crow*, if not to its conclusions. The language has a fastidious, at times arctic, sensuality and the mythic-archetypal dimension serves as a compressor rather than a pump. Harsent's creatures, human and otherwise, lead not to allegorical flatness and abstraction but to the further interior of their world.

Punch, as the quotation indicates, is a closed system: incorrigible, conspiratorial, leering, paterfamilial, triumphant and, in the intervals of his sexual adventures, horrified by what his behaviour may signify. Above all he is immutable in the cycles of his conduct – and irredeemably male, the imprisoned celebrant of the scopophilic gaze. While Harsent gives few indications of period, Punch's interior theatre of desires has points in common with the mad and fearful world to which the black comedy of Martin Amis's *Dead Babies* introduces us: "His mind comes loose: he sees a figure / out on the drowning streets, // camouflaged by morning twilight, / watching the room, his eyes / luminous, like an assassin's. / Her shadow runs on the curtain, then she floats, / a tangle of pink and gold on frosted glass."

As with Amis, the question of misogyny arises. In Harsent's case, it seems fair to say that misogyny is part of the subject of the work rather than a condition indulged by the authorial imagination, although this imagination was shaped in the pre-feminist era and is less concerned with a direct moral examination of misogyny than with its impact on the experience of those who look and those who are looked at. Elsewhere in Harsent's work, in the series of Stella Mooney crime novels he published as David Lawrence, a powerful, active female figure is brought to the fore. Yet Mooney is very clearly a male version of female competence and control, and the West London world of feral estates and bedsits in which she moves is seen with a disquieting vividness which is very much the author's.

In his wonderful early poem 'April on Toronto Island', Derek Mahon speaks of "our lives in infinite preparation", and as Harsent moved into the 1990s there was a sense that while he had a body of impressive and satisfying work to his name, there was an element in the offing which he had yet to fully identify. He has commented that his poems "are written out of a compulsion that I recognize but don't fully (and don't care to) understand", so that we may infer that the pursuit of self-knowledge is not the purpose of the work – an interpretation borne out by the sense that even in autobiographical-seeming early work such as 'Haircut', 'Terms' or 'Retreat', the sense of exposure is offset by an equal sense of anonymity. We might trace the influence here of poems by Robert Lowell, such as 'Marriage', 'My Old Flame' and 'Water', but whereas Lowell gives off a sense that the events described are important because they happened to *him*, in Harsent's case the importance lies in the fact that they are happening to *someone*. He stands, perhaps, in the Confessional tradition, but without feeling obliged to own up to anything specific: this is the confessional form as fiction.

In the event, the next important developments to occur in Harsent's work were in the first place formal rather than thematic. A poem such as 'Coverack', from the 1998 collection *A Bird's Idea of Flight*, reveals a new expansiveness, an ease among unfurling sentences, an avoidance of the clipped authority which might have become an imprisoning mannerism. As a result, the poems begin to let their strange world breathe a little more. In this enigmatic narrative, encounters with a hare (the most potent of animals for Harsent's imagination) and an Ancient Mariner figure with "his eyes / like peeled eggs and his mossy smile" leads to a visit to a sunken wreck and then a glimpse of the shore:

> Salt and sunlight gave it a grainy bloom,
> the colour pretty much gone from everything,
> white trees, white hills, white stones in the harbour wall,
> white buildings, my wife's white face, white faces
> of my children staring out across the bay
> as if they might catch my eye,
> already whitened by sunlight and salt,
> between an acre of sea and an acre of sky.

We can also hear, latterly, the emergence of rhyme, to which Harsent had not previously given his full allegiance, alongside an intensification of rhythm to rather eerie effect. At times the effect blends incantation with interrogation, when the dead sailor enquires of the narrator:

> 'Did someone you love
> ever die, or else did you wish
> someone would? Did you ever come to grief
> thanks to a lie? Did your hand

> ever cheat your eye? Did you ever
> long for the sea as you might have longed for your bed?'

The peremptory force of this sinister near-nonsense seems to penetrate the narrator's fragile assurance, to visit on him a debt of guilt simply for being on hand – an effect which anticipates the folkloric nightmare of Don Paterson's 'The Blue Flower'. In both cases it is as though consciousness itself becomes unappeasably punitive.

In itself Harsent's concern with the visible would be unremarkable – since Romanticism in particular the visible world has absorbed many English poets – but his visual attentiveness is at once too deliberate and involuntary, even driven, to be merely a sign of cultural habit. Fiercely rich in colour, his world is often exact and hard-edged, yet at times its charged particulars look as if about to metamorphose. It can seem voyeuristic: the imagination engaged by curiosity, yet withheld in a kind of connoisseurial privacy, as though seeing is separated from what (including persons) is seen. We might follow a line of condemnatory argument from this point, but it's more interesting to consider what faith Harsent places in the visible world, whether the world itself or as depicted in art. Whatever cannot be known, he suggests, can still be *seen clearly*. This is a central factor in *Marriage* (2002), the book which brought Harsent a new level of attention. The poet notes that the book is "very loosely" based on the relationship between the painter Pierre Bonnard and Marthe Meligny, his muse and model, whom he married only to discover that he had not even known her real name. As always, Harsent keeps his options open: the poems are not to become auxiliary to their source – a danger not always avoided in contemporary poetry, when hunger for extended subjects sometimes leads to the sacrifice of the poems' autonomy. *Marriage* is not 'really' about Bonnard and Meligny; nor is it a personal confession. The poems are at once intimate and aware of intimacy's limits, as in v:

> Have you put a touch of auburn to your hair? That's new.
> It helps. So does the dab of blusher and lip-
> gloss: 'Carmensita'; now, if I look hard, it's you
>
> and not you, playing slip-
> the-noose in a swarm of dapple by our geranium wall.
> How is it you know me so well if I scarcely know you at all?

This is what happens to the love-lyric after the invention of the realist novel and cinema: details drive out generality, disguising to an extent the fact that this is just as much a petition as 'Go, Lovely Rose', the difference being that in a sense that beloved has no choice but in Waller's phrase to "suffer herself to be desired", as a condition of a love to which her own commitment may prove to be ambiguous: "you know me so well" may bespeak her exhausted familiarity as much as the imaginative generosity for which men depend so heavily on women. While beginning to trace these possibilities in the poem it's important not to neglect its lightness of touch in blending the 'work' of observation with the disquiet that resides in the familiar. This marks a considerable advance on 'Dreams of the Dead' and 'Mr Punch': whereas they seem somehow drawn to a suggestive stasis, *Marriage* lives in the act of discovery and the signs of change from moment to moment.

What *Marriage* does for the erotic dimension of Harsent's work *Legion* (2005) does for violence. The book imagines the effort to hear and bring to mind and interpret events, rumours and silent pauses which it might often seem wiser or saner to let go of, were that possible. The savagery of *Legion*'s world clearly owes much to the Balkan wars of the 1990s, which Harsent had addressed earlier in his translations from the poet Goran Simić, in *The Sorrows of Sarajevo* and *Sprinting from the Graveyard*. From time to time the media asks where the contemporary war poets are. In the absence of a world conflict requiring a mass mobilization of the British population, Harsent's grim echo-chamber of horrors is an impressive contemporary version. The title itself evokes the story of the Gadarene swine in the Gospel of St. Mark, where Jesus approaches the possessed man and asks: "What is thy name? And he answered, saying, My name is Legion: for we are many." It is not that Harsent entertains the notion of supernatural demonic possession, rather that the behaviour encouraged and legitimized in a war zone, particularly where religion and ethnicity are involved, takes on a character for which secular moral categories seem inadequate, where "man is a wolf to man" and to woman and child as well.

Legion grimly demonstrates the human capacity to exceed what is ordinarily thinkable, at the same time as reminding us that this is familiar European terrain and that barely sixty years separate us from the daily indulgence of such behaviour. In 'Ghost Archaeology' investigators come on evidence of atrocity: "the buckram-bound ledgers... the data. / Such orthodoxies there, such wheels within wheels, / such a rich and full account of the dark desiderata." The sumptuousness of the utterance, in particular of the rhyme, is both impressive and troubling. In one sense Harsent's view is

Manichean; in another it is holistic, proposing that an acknowledgment of our brutal capacities is a necessary though imperfect condition for trying to avoid their recurrence. The demonic other is, potentially, ourselves and our neighbours. Peacetime, when the wreck of material life – its walls and fireplaces, chairs and dolls and fish-slices – is repaired and repainted, must not consist of forgetting, though it probably will, when the conflict is gradually assigned to that vague elsewhere in which such things happen, since clearly they cannot happen here. For Harsent, though, there is no enclave called 'here', no haven, a fact which vindicates his presentation of a world both richly detailed and crucially unspecific. Here could be anywhere, over the hills or down the neighbouring street. This is as close to politics as he comes.

With *Night*, his ninth full collection, Harsent appears to return to the private sphere, often to a back garden at the gateway hours of dusk or dawn, a place where society is a rumour and where the brooding mind inextricably mingles the inner and outer worlds: "Yourself at the very point / where what's yours bleeds off through the palings / to *terra incognita*". The vision of the wheel of fortune in 'Rota Fortunae' offers a sense akin to the account given by Virgil in *Inferno* Canto VIII that the structures we erect are not the true order of the world, that society dissolves to reveal the fates of individuals, that there is no leave to appeal. Virgil, Dante's companion, describes the workings of Fortune as both "beyond all human wit to intervene" and wholly reasonable, as the will of God is reasonable. In place of divine punishment or reward, Harsent emphasizes the brutality of chance: "that note you sang was the voices of those on the wheel // teased out to a single sound that might have chilled / the blood of a man less troubled; and all the while / they were singing it back to you, or singing it back to the wind." The "you" of the poem, waking before dawn, startled by the flight of a bird, experiences that renewed apprehension of the world which is often thought of as the effect of art. Yet in this case no emancipation from care is on offer, only Lowell's "blessed structures, plot and rhyme", as Harsent's endlessly ingenious, heavily-enjambed triplets promise the authority of *terza rima* without ever settling into it. The beauty of the writing is both a gift and a goad.

'Ghosts' employs the same form across a single twenty-seven-line sentence, some of whose terrain is likewise Dantesque – "its undrinkable rivers, its scrubland of snarls and hooks" recalling the wood of suicides in Canto XIII. Harsent's "you", though, is no Dante and has no Virgil to act as psychopomp in the mind's underworld. When Dante encounters his teacher Brunetto Latini in Canto XV, there is a gladness of recognition amid the horror of Brunetto's fate, but Harsent's speaker/addressee cannot muster the generosity to convert self-knowledge into love or escape a bottomless solitude: the ghosts come "bearing a look / of matchless sorrow as would, for sure, / stop the heart of whoever it is they take you for". In one sense the speaker resembles Auden's citizen who finds that his request to suffer has been refused, in this case by his own temperament; in another, the denial of recognition to the ghosts is a sign of deep damnation in the imprisoning ego. And either way the ghosts cannot be released from their haunting task, because without recognition there is nowhere for them to go back to. The "familiar compound ghost" of Eliot's *Little Gidding* is here reduced to a crowd of supplicants.

In *Night* Harsent shows an affinity with an apparently rather different poet, Peter Porter, who also wrote of what he called "the thousand green horrors, the self", and of "the smell of self", and visited the border-zone of the psyche and the underworld in poems of elegy and guilt such as the magnificent and terrible 'The Delegate' from *The Cost of Seriousness*, in which the poet is addressed by his dead wife in terms which offer a truth but no succour. It's hard to find a more complimentary comparison. Porter and Harsent have a dramatizing power in common, and although Porter speaks of "lyrical erotica I have no talent for", which is clearly part of Harsent's territory, and seems conscientiously to evade the arrow-sure mellifluousness of Harsent's mature work, both poets share the conviction of Marlow in *Heart of Darkness* that "We live as we dream – alone." Indeed, in Harsent's work, the sphere of human relationships – the lit room, the glimpsed kitchen, the garden, the female figures – often seems to lie close at hand yet out of reach, with the poems' characters both present and not-there in their own lives. In the painterly 'Vanitas', a seated male figure watching a woman watching him in a mirror strikes a note of black humour: "This is a lesson, I think, in how to feel", before concluding that the room is "a wilderness". The grotesque 'Spatchcock', where a woman boning a chicken and a masterful Bond-figure having sex with her are allowed to blend into each other, portrays a monstrous male vanity which would be beyond the reach of pathos were it not laughably anachronistic, the sort of thing the late George Macbeth might, not quite in earnest, have come up with. A telling and chilling line in the early poem 'Haircut' states, "We have learned to pretend that we live like this", which might function as an epigraph for much of the mature work, too. It is the nature of the mind, Harsent suggests, always to be on the wrong side of the glass – looking in, looking out, looking back, but unable to look away, able to create order but never to assuage the ills it brings to coherence.

Night concludes with the near-epic dream-vision 'Elsewhere', Harsent's most extended visit to his contemporary underworld, which strikes a masterly balance between the compelling moment and the necessary momentum of the whole, modulating from a noirish milieu of liquor and basement grot to the sea shore, and to the impulse to make a song out of what seems to be a curse made of "the long slow haul / from loving to leaving" and "all the luck / falling to either the monstrous or the moonstruck":

> [...] That was a time of trial.
> That was when we lived life on the fly:
> nothing slow or solemn, nothing dark or deep.
> Everything I got I got by guile; everything I had was mine to keep.

How much the scale of Harsent's seriousness has grown; the clever, slightly laddish hermeticism of some of the early work seems a very long time ago. In its place we witness the steady exploration of the far interior of an imaginative world which is unmistakeably unique to the author, where an exact lyricism is matched to a circling obsession with matters which are finally unspeakable, more elegant than Berryman, less diaristic than Lowell, fit company for either. Harsent is a decade and more older than those contemporary poets with whom he has the clearest affinities – Robin Robertson, Jo Shapcott and Don Paterson: he links them to the severe lyricism of his late friend Ian Hamilton and shows it to have had far greater imaginative potential than many might have supposed, bringing a distinctive inflection to the post-religious concern with Last Things which characterizes the younger poets. Perhaps the test of a poet's importance is whether he has the authority to make his subject matter indisputably ours as well. In this Harsent has surely succeeded, and the mapping of his grimly beautiful terrain is far from complete.

Sean O'Brien's *November* is a PBS Choice and shortlisted for the T.S. Eliot Prize.

English Language Writing By Indian Poets

British poetry has long been enriched by writers with an Indian background, from Sujata Bhatt to Debjani Chatterjee, Daljit Nagra to Amarjit Chandan and Imtiaz Dharker. *Poetry Review* has decided to explore some of the related work that, because it isn't written in the UK, is less accessible for British readers.

Sudeep Sen, who researched the material for this feature and provided the biographical notes, all of which are extracted from a major forthcoming anthology, writes:

This selection, taken from the forthcoming *The HarperCollins Book of English Poetry by Indians*, which I am engaged in editing, concentrates largely on poets who use, or experiment with, formal verse structures, and those who also have a strong British link. As well as the sonnet, forms include: rubai, ghazal, triolet, Sapphic fragments, Bhartrhari-style shataka, prose poetry, and mosaic pastiche.

ARUNDHATHI SUBRAMANIAM writes poetry, edits the India domain of Holland's *Poetry International Web*, and writes on culture. She is the author of three books of poetry: *On Cleaning Bookshelves* (Allied), *Where I Live* (Allied), and *New and Selected Poems* (Bloodaxe). She has co-edited an anthology of Indian love poems in English, *Confronting Love* (Penguin), an anthology of nonsense verse, *A Pocket Full of Wry* (Penguin forthcoming), and the *2010 Commonwealth Games Indian Poetry Anthology* (Sahitya Akademi). Anthology appearances include: *The Literary Review Indian Poetry* (New Jersey: Fairleigh Dickinson University), *The Yellow Nib Contemporary English Poetry by Indians* (Belfast: Queens University), *World Literature Today Writing from Modern India* (Norman: University of Oklahoma), all edited by Sudeep Sen. She is also the author of a prose work, *The Book of Buddha* (Penguin). She curated 'Chauraha', an interactive arts forum at Mumbai's National Centre for the Performing Arts, for several years. She writes regularly on literature, dance and spirituality for various publications; and lives in Mumbai.

Epigrams For Life After Forty

Between the doorbell
and the death knell
is the tax exemption certificate.

There are fewer capital letters
than we supposed.

Other people's stories will do.
Sticky nougatine green-and-pink stories.
Other people's stories.

Untenanting is more difficult
than unbelonging.

The body? The same alignment
of flesh, bone, the scent of soap, yesterday's
headlines, a soupçon of opera.

But there *are* choices
other than cringing vassal state
and walled medieval town.

And there is a language
of aftermath,
a language of ocean and fluttering sail,
of fishing villages malabared
by palm, and dreams laced
with arrack and moonlight.

And it can even be
enough.

BHANU KAPIL was born in England in 1968, to Indian parents, and grew up in a working-class, South-Asian community in Greater London. She went to the U.S. in 1990 and currently lives in Boulder, Colorado, where she teaches at Naropa University. A writer forged by this history of migration who has come to understand the border as a site of both transformation and loss, Kapil's work crosses genre and subject borders. Her books include: *Autobiography of a Cyborg* (2000), *The Vertical Interrogation of Strangers* (2001) and *Incubation: A Space for Monsters* (2006). Anthology appearances include: *The Yellow Nib Contemporary English Poetry by Indians*. She has recently completed a long prose work, *Humanimal: a project for future children*, a creative non-fiction account of the Wolfgirls of Midnapure, two children found living with wolves in 1920s Bengal.

from 1. Schizophrene

I threw the book into the dark garden. The account begun mid-ocean, in a storm.

*

Immigrant. Nothing happens. *Immigrant.*

*

Below the aeroplane is the river.

*

Someone who could weight me down, whether physically or with language, in all the ports of call: Athens in January, Munich in February, London in March! Immigrant, there's nothing erotic about the ten rupees in your pocket. The account begins mid-ocean, where even your boarding pass is knotted in a handkerchief in your broken-down suitcase in the hold. Dazzling you, I select your suitcase. You watch it float over the railing and into the air. Yellow lightning in the silver sky, and the three sheets of rain, so bamboo, so cream. Stupid man, you watch your suitcase sink, burning up its requisite energy simply by breathing. Everything breathes, even you. Breathe, immigrant. Fly, immigrant. Sail, immigrant. Blue.

*

When I opened the door, there was a weird blue light coming off the snow. I threw the book into the snow.

*

The ship left Bombay at dawn, a pink smear, the sunlight both a position and an entity.

*

The ship docked. The ferry left Calais at dawn, a green sky, I kept drawing the horizon, the static line somehow disc-like.

Near seven, I saw an intense set of orange, red and gold lines above the place where the sun would be.

The ship docked, and I found my home in the grid system: the damp wooden stool in the bath, a slice of bread with cheese on it, and so on. All my life, I've been trying to adhere to the surface of your city, your three grey rectangles split into four parts; a red dot; the axis rotated seventy-six degrees, and so on.

*

But then I threw the book into the grid. It was a wet grid.

*

The snow wet the book then froze it like a passive sun. These notes are directed towards the region I wanted to perceive, but could not. Notes for a schizophrene night, a schizophrene day, a rapid sketch.

*

The book before writing, arcing once more through the crisp dark air. And the line the book makes is an axis, a hunk of electromagnetic fur torn from the side of something still living and thrown, like a wire, threaded, a spark towards the grass.

*

A line for someone on their first voyage, a non-contemporary subject, the woman, or even the man, the person with an articulate gender, a flux where the body always is, who asks what's forbidden and what's expected in the annular zone. In the airport. On the earth.
A veil. A harness. A rope.

Do psychiatrists register the complex and rich vibrations produced by their dreaming subjects? The indigo or emerald-green *crown* that coats the hair and shoulders of an *interviewee*, erasing distinctions between what is outside, the sky, and what's beneath it? That digs into the head?

The "emanating structures appear in the light that comes from the body, and it is these structures that perform a rudimentary narrative." *A memory or two?*

*

Writing, I notice that the schizophrenic narrative is not split, for which an antidote is commercially produced in quantities that exceed populations. Rather, it cannot process the dynamic elements of an image, any image, whether pleasant, enriching or already so bad it can't be tendered in the lexicon of poses available to it.

I need a new pen.

*

An idea for a novel before it's shattered, there on the bench next to the fountain, which is frozen, deconstructed, in the air.

*

I walk the long way to the Tate from the Pimlico tube, a fact more intense each time I repeat it in my mind. An erotics. A mad progression that exceeds a central frame, like seeing something then falling down.

I break my walk at the fountain, as I've done since childhood, which is chromatography. The white panels, then a livid black.

It's already late. A black world coming down from the heavens. Black with stars.

*

They're walking into that, the darkness pouring into their mouths when they reach the hills. Coming down over the two of them: a man of about sixty, that red afternoon into evening, the dirt of that place a kind of orange-brown, and his grand-daughter, eight years old that July. A Londoner, she's wearing a blue and yellow dress with a daisy print. As for the man, he's dressed in a white cotton dhoti and a kurta, with an almond-cake pale shawl, embroidered along its narrow border with maroon and turquoise paisley swirls.

*

The upwelling of philosophy attends to what we can't see. A light tent over the text.

[...]

KARTHIKA NAIR was born in Kottyam in the southern Indian state of Kerala. As a child of an Indian Army officer, she moved and lived in many different Indian cities and states such as Delhi, Kolkata, Assam, Kerala, Meghalaya, and Uttar Pradesh. She moved to France in 2000 to pursue a master's degree in art management, and stayed on in Paris thereafter, where she has worked for institutions like the Grande Halle de la Villette, the Cité de la musique, and the Centre national de la danse. In 2007 she switched sides to manage choreographer Sidi Larbi Cherkaoui's projects. Her poems have appeared in *Atlas, Indian Literature, Saint-Denis, portraits sensibles,* among others. Anthology appearances include: *The Literary Review Indian Poetry,* and *The Yellow Nib Contemporary English Poetry by Indians.* Her first book of poetry, *Bearings,* appeared from HarperCollins India in 2009. She lives and works in Paris.

Two Triolets

1. Montreal: Fall

Tell me it must be the weather
that dyes my mind white, congeals thought –
not meltdown of that myth: *Together.*
Tell me it must be the weather
not your ire, nor eyes that ether
memory, blaze the words we wrought –
tell me! It must be the weather
that dies: minds in flight can seal thought.

2. Rome: Winter

We drove to Rome to unreel pride
and pain, staunch the blame, drain dissent,
graft content. The last galactic tide:
we drove to Rome to anneal pride
with 'art and rain. When the Tiber died –
riven blue-black by rage misspent –
we drove from Rome to unreel, ride
the pain, staunch the blame... feign consent.

MICHELLE CAHILL is Goan-Anglo-Indian. She wrote *The Accidental Cage*, shortlisted in the 2007 Judith Wright Poetry Prize. She was highly commended in the 2009 Blake Poetry Prize, the Alec Bolton Prize and the Inverawe Poetry Prize. *Vishvarupa*, her second poetry collection, themed around Hindu gods, is forthcoming soon. Anthology appearances include: *The Yellow Nib Contemporary English Poetry by Indians* and *World Literature Today Writing from Modern India*. She writes fiction and essays and has been awarded grants from the Australia Council, the Copyright Agency Limited and the Australian Society of Authors. She co-edits the online magazine, *Mascara Literary Review*.

Kali From Abroad

Kali, you are the poster-goddess, sticking out your black
tongue, like Gene Simmons from Kiss, a kick in the teeth,
with your punk-blue leggings, your skull and scissor charms.

You swing a trident, a demon's head and dance on the bones
of a pale Shiva. I recall the convincing eyes of a girl cripple
carrying your bottled effigy, as our bus careened to a dusty halt.

Some say you morphed from Parvati, drunk on blood,
others cite your superhero leap from Durga's brow to slay
the self-cloning serpent before a Haka dance on mythic soil.

By a hundred Sanskrit names, India claims you in a single text,
while in *Zen and the Art of Motorcycle Maintenance*, you are
'the grass and the dew', on screen, our contemporary Judge Judy

having a bad hair day. I'd argue for your cosmopolitanism,
a global denizen, you're adroit in drugs and aphrodisiacs, a nude
Dominatrix, a feminist export with a sadomasochistic bent.

A figure of partition you were cover girl for *Time* magazine.
A Neo-pagan diva, your wholeness is darkness fashioned
from light, moon-breasted, with eyes of fire, with Brahma's feet,

Varuna's watery thighs. You rise from the grave, step over
carnage, feeding the world and your severed self with blood.
Stripped bare as Duchamp's Bride, you set Bachelors in motion.

RUKMINI BHAYA NAIR was born in 1952. She was educated in Calcutta and
then went on to receive a PhD from Cambridge University. Nair specialises in
cognitive linguistics and critical theory, and her books in these areas include:
Narrative Gravity, *Technobrat*, and *Lying on the Postcolonial Couch*. Winner of
numerous awards and honours, she has published three collections of
poetry: *The Hyoid Bone*, *The Ayodhya Cantos* and *Yellow Hibiscus*. Anthology
appearances include: *Midnight's Grandchildren: Post Independence Poetry
from India* (Macedonia: Struga Poetry Evenings) and *World Literature Today
Writing from Modern India*. She is on the editorial boards of the *International
Journal of Literary Semantics* and *Biblio*; as well as the advisory panel of the
Macmillan Essential Dictionary. Nair is Professor of Linguistics and English
at the Department of Humanities and Social Sciences, Indian Institute of
Technology, New Delhi.

from SHATAKA: Mourning The Mumbai Massacre

The terrible calamity

No invocation, this, but terror's end foretold...
Listen, Bhartrhari, let me be whorish frank with you – those fine
Sanskrit words of yours, *niti sringara vairagya* whatnot – they
Mean damn all when ten boys with guns come blasting through
No, not at pheasants, their brown, cocked heads drooping
And the bejewelled azure of the sky vanishing in a mini-second
From the round-bead droplets of their startled eyes, the feathers
A corona of tiny fireworks illuminating death at noonday
That bow-and-arrows murder would be bad enough but what we saw
After the world's recent burning, Bhartrhari, could your 6th century wit
Encompass? I think not, somehow. I think rain. I just *think rain*, desperate.

*

When a stranger walks into the rain-forest's glisten, should a madwoman follow?
Another thing, Bhartrhari, I'll have to keep this short, no more than
Ten lines per poem, because it's obvious I'm losing it. My saris hang
Unwashed, hair falls in my cold tea in clumps and nobody knocks ever
Which surely is not *vairagya* as you conceived it – that dignified walk
Into a forest glade renouncing the world's sparkling medallions
Venison banquets, silk robes and that sudden tumescence when you spotted
The vermillion in her adulterous tresses, how could this ascetic role
Be mine? Who am I to mourn, to expiate, who has given up nothing, but
Whom everyone else has given up on entirely, which is not surprising –
My so-called poetry is such bilious trash. Here, judge for yourself!

*

[...]

*

When I mention the disturbance of the crows, you nod, thinking it a bad
omen – but...

The rest seems barbarous Greek to you! O Bharthari, my guru, I sense
The logician's annoyance rising in you – as if it is Ujjaini's holy river
pierced

By a million August spikes of rain and bleeding copious onto its banks
A caulked stag in the King's brutal hunt – and yet this same Ganga
returns

Healed, each miraculous spring! It is immortal, men are not, that's
The pity of it, Bharati, as you say. *The silence of a river salves its wounds*
But the words of men destroy, they are a guide to foolishness, so how can I
Possibly explain to you my bludgeoning Anglo-Saxon words, my
battering rams

Of acronyms – TV, NSG, SMS, WMDs and others still lurking perfidious
Behind an enemy arras such as VIP and VOIP – oh innocent Polonius-
Bharata…

*

How can I ever transmit to you the unspeakable lexicon of my century?
Faridkot then – let's begin easy with Faridkot, although the odd
Thing is that they disown Aamir Kasab entirely there – but, being mortal
He has to come from somewhere – so let's say he comes from this small
Green village far from your own arid domain, the black stony soil of
Malwa

Where only bajra and sorghum grew – *what, what did you say?* I didn't
quite

Catch it. Oh, you're saying I've got things wrong! Do I mean *Sialkot*, not
Faridkot? You've not heard of this Aamer or of his obscure village
But Sialkot now – it was famous, almost as famous as your own Ujjaini
Sialkot stood where Menander ruled, rich Greek satrapy of second century
Outer limit of Alexander's great Bactrian state… But before that *rain…*

---

from AUTHOR NOTE:

> Bhartrhari: (born 570? Ujjain, Malwa, India, died 651? Ujjain) Indian Hindu philosopher, poet, and grammarian [...] *Vakyapadiya* is his major work on the philosophy of language. Also ascribed to him are three collections of poetry, each containing one hundred verses: *Shrngara-shataka* (on love), *Niti-shataka* (on ethics and polity) and *Vairagya-shataka* (on dispassion). His poem *Bhatti kavya* demonstrates the subtleties of Sanskrit.
>
> – www.servinghistory.com/topics/Bhartrhari

What could be more innocuous than the enterprise of reading a sixth century grammarian, one might have thought. But how [...] could I ever explain to someone like Bhartrhari – who lived in an age before mobile phones, automatic weapons and RDX, not to mention academic women with spectacles perched on their noses earnestly typing away at luminous computer screens – what modern terrorism amounts to? In the process of this confused questioning, I discovered, too, that Bhartrhari was a near contemporary of the Prophet Muhammad, also born in the sixth century. How would these wise erudite figures from the past have conversed with each other? [...] I wanted to write a collection of Bhartrhari-style *shataka* (the word means 'one hundred') that attempted to convey to the sharpest of pre-modern minds some of the most intractable of the dilemmas confronting us in the fraught twenty-first century. Below, following initiatory quotations from the Holy Koran and Bhartrhari's verse, are the first nine poems of this – not sonnet but *shataka* – sequence.

Sudeep Sen's books include: *Postmarked India: New & Selected Poems* (HarperCollins), *Prayer Flag* (Peepal Tree), *Rain* (Gallerie), *Aria* (Mulfran), *The HarperCollins Book of English Poetry by Indians* (editor); and *Atlas*, www.atlasaarkarts.net

The Light Touch

STEPHEN KNIGHT

Arun Kolatkar, *Collected Poems in English*, ed. Arvind Krishna Mehrotra, Bloodaxe, £12, ISBN

Born in Kolhapur, India in 1931, the bilingual poet Arun Kolatkar – who had, his editor notes, "an inexplicable dread of publishers' contracts" – released just three books of poetry in English in his lifetime, the first, *Jejuri*, in 1976, the others in 2004, the year of his death. Elusive, gifted with the lightest of touches, Kolatkar is fond of the monologue, quirkily voicing, among other things, a stray mongrel and an old bicycle tyre. His droll manner is always present. The dog, for example, traces its ancestry back to the hounds brought over from England

> by Sir Bartle Frere
> in eighteen hundred and sixty-four
> with the crazy idea
>
> of introducing fox-hunting to Bombay.
> Just the sort of thing
> he felt the city badly needed.

Reading as if composed on the spot, Kolatkar's poems are akin to the very best of American poetry – he favours words like "goofed" and "schmuck" – in that they are in the moment and wonderfully attentive, recording the fleetingness of a butterfly, a woman picking lice from her lover's head, an infant being bathed, and a crow swooping to an object in the road "until you just skim along, / give yourself a slight lift, / and touch down. // Oh, that was just beautifully done / – you, you, you / airdevil!" His comprehensive tone can conjure trees at dawn, which "arrive at themselves / each one ready / to give an account of its leaves," or deploy a word like "*keer-e-khar*", which, a note informs us, is "Persian for donkey's dick."

While *Jejuri* finds the sacred and the profane together in a Maharashtran pilgrim town's fallen pillars, sleepy railway station and a patched-up cupboard full of gold gods in tidy rows, many of the subjects for Kolatkar's other poems are observed from his table at the Wayside Inn, as if to demonstrate the truth of James Schuyler's notion that it should be possible to start poems simply by looking out of a window. And what a window Kolatkar found! Taken in its entirety, his work is not just a capturing of moments and things with precision and detail – the eyelets of a tarpaulin, the hairs in a nostril, "a sari wears a grin / where your buttocks have sucked it in" – but the unsentimental portrait of a community, especially in the tour de force 'Breakfast Time at Kala Ghoda', its one hundred and ninety-seven unrhymed triplets (a favourite stanza form of Kolatkar's) bringing to brilliant life his corner of the planet.

Collected Poems in English must already be regarded a classic of English language poetry from India. In time, if there is any justice, its reputation will cross the globe.

Stephen Knight's book for children, *Sardines and Other Poems*, was published in 2004.

REVIEWS

There is an exhilaration about reading
certain poets whose powers continue
to heighten with age.

– *W.N. Herbert*

Homegrown And Exiled

CAROL RUMENS

Iain Crichton Smith, *New Collected Poems*, ed. Matthew McGuire,
Carcanet, £18.95, ISBN 9781857549607;
Ian Duhig, *Pandorama*, Picador, £8.99, ISBN 9780330521246

This *New Collected Poems* by Iain Crichton Smith (1928-1998) updates and expands the *Collected Poems* of 1992. Matthew McGuire adds a considerable amount of fresh material, including extracts from the 1971 translation of Sorley MacLean's epic, *Dàin do Eimhir agus Dàin Eile* (1943) and valuable work from Smith's four late collections, all published in the 1990s.

A prolific novelist as well as poet, Smith was born in Glasgow in 1928. When he was two years old, he moved with his mother to the Hebridean island of Lewis. Education distanced him from the Gaelic language he spoke at home: he attended Aberdeen University to study English Literature, and went on to become a school-teacher. His home for most of his life was in the Scottish Highlands. Exile, both geographical and linguistic, is a central theme of his work, but an equally fruitful argument in Smith's imaginative dialectic is between the narrow discipline preached by the Free Presbyterian Church and the creative natural life Smith valued as an artist. This conflict obsesses him to the end, expressed even in the symbolism of "the leaf and the marble" of the 1998 sequence, whose setting is contemporary Rome. The island of Lewis, though a harsh foster-mother, taught Smith to fuse the visionary and the realistic. The beautiful early 'Poem of Lewis' fingers the wound exactly:

> They have no place for the fine graces
> of poetry. The great forgiving spirit of the word
> fanning its rainbow wing, like a shot bird
> falls from the windy sky. The sea heaves
> in visionless anger over the cramped graves
> and the early daffodil, purer than a soul,
> is gathered into the terrible mouth of the gale.

Smith is equally at ease with the staple metres of English poetry as with free-er verse. His poems absorb a wide range of literature, exploring the

European canon and beyond (Virgil, Dante, Marcus Aurelius, Shakespeare), not as a scholar but as an intensely responsive reader: "No library that I haven't loved. / My food is books." Some of the earlier work has an Audenesque flavour: "Children, follow the dwarves, and the giants, and the wolves / into the Wood of Unknowing, into the leaves // where the terrible granny perches and sings to herself / past the tumultuous seasons, high on her shelf." There are many terrible grannies in these poems, typically less archetypal than here though, and portrayed with a richer awareness of their individuality and stoicism.

Imagery leads abstract thought towards the surreal at times: "It was the heavy jokes, the dreadful jokes, / the pewter-coloured jokes that drove you mad"; "Do colours cry? Does 'black' weep for the dead?" Those last rhetorical questions are from *Deer on the High Hills*, a powerful, closely-knit series of poems whose firm triplet stanzas combine a Gaelic rhetorical 'lift' with metaphysical wit: "The deer step out in isolated air. / The cloud is cloudy and the word wordy. / Winter is wintry, lonely is your journey." Smith enjoyed the expansive, meditative opportunities of the sequence: another important one, *The White Air of March*, has a more Modernist verse-structure, fragmented and angular. There's a lovely moment when, shifting scale from the Cuillin mountain-landscape and the lofty poetic aspiration it inspires ("The music of the imagination must be restored / upward"), he casts an amused and tender eye toward "The little Highland dancer / in white shirt, green kilt," as she skips between swords, watching out for her toes.

Smith's darker moods are balanced by this generous imagination and open mind. He can mock the pedantries of Gaelic scholarship, and deliver an affectionately revisionist pat to McGonagall. He is not primarily a landscape artist but a poet of the "man-made," surprised by the almost-joy of cities, schools, football stadia and above all people, the very young and very old in particular. One of his last poems, 'The Poet', might be his own elegy:

> I have outdistanced the music
> I am travelling in silence
> through the shadow of posthumous metres.
>
> What my metres will be
> will be what I shall become –
>
> I am the skin-made drum
>
> which the wind will fill.

This magnificent *Collected* will ensure Smith's music is carried to the future.

Ian Duhig, born in London of Irish parents, is now an adopted Loiner (Leeds person). His new collection, *Pandorama*, appropriately signals a debt to Tony Harrison: the form-fastened rage against class injustice, the Rhubarbarian fascination with language and etymology. But Duhig's persona is less edgy: language as a game is one of the enabling insights of the literary theory inherited by poets born in the 1950s. Harrison, with his "little stick of Leeds-grown tusky", in fact gets gently teased at the close of 'Unmaking', where the wild boar are whispering "Tusky tusky which means nothing." The class migration which is registered somewhat guiltily by Harrison, and implicated in Smith's painful sense of exile, is a joyous resource for Duhig, celebrated in historical excavations and eclectic "book-learning".

The tightly constructed 'Ribblehead' (VI of the bravura sequence *Jericho Shanty*) mirrors with a shiver the brickwork of the Ribblehead Viaduct, in the construction of which one navvy is said to have died for every brick laid. The workmen were frequently told to "go to Jericho", i.e. to get lost:

> acid rain
>   owl light
> polished plate
>   foul bite
>
> under the bridgework,
>   teeth of air
> navvies whistle
>   elsewhere

And the collection takes its title from Robert Tressell's *The Ragged Trousered Philanthropists*, a novel intended to be "a faithful picture of working-class life – more especially of those engaged in the building trades". One of its characters, Bert White, builds a "World-famous Pandorama", a wooden box with rollers that unfurl a moving ribbon of pictures, carefully pasted together to form a political commentary – grotesque, bloody, hilarious – as these poems often are. But the workman's panoramic show is not only scenic: it's accompanied by children singing ironically appropriate music-hall ditties, with the audience joining in the chorus. And it's the singable, if sometimes twelve-tone, music of Duhig's book that makes it special and memorable, whether the poem is a ballad, or a Muldoonian list forged into an angry elegy for David Oluwale, the Nigerian immigrant hounded to death by policemen

('Via Negativa'), or the Henry Newbolt super-skit, 'Braque's Drum'. The collection is itself a large-scale sequence, connecting Freemasons and stonemasons, boxers and boxes, unreliable narrators and thesis-writers, *et al.*

Post-modern knock-about comedy may never be too far away, but the last lines of the book's last poem, 'Lying Over the Ground', lead us almost back to Iain Crichton Smith:

> To poets and their readers, words are grace;
> their roads best taken at an easy pace,
> while even better than an easy pace is
> entropy, collapse, then total stasis –
> lots of poets write their best in bed:
> the truly great among them are all dead.

These two collections illuminate the sea-change that's occurred in English, Scottish and Irish poetry in fewer than thirty years. But you don't need to make an un-Free Presbyterian choice between good and evil, one or the other. Both are authentic, both are necessary: buy them!

Carol Rumens's most recent collection is *De Chirico's Threads* (2010).

Enough Is As Good As A Feast

STEVEN MATTHEWS

August Kleinzahler, *Sleeping It Off in Rapid City: New and Selected Poems*,
Faber, £12.99, ISBN 9780571260119;
Glyn Maxwell, *One Thousand Nights and Counting: Selected Poems*,
Picador, £14.99, ISBN 9780330534406;
Michael McClure, *Of Indigo and Saffron: New and Selected Poems*,
University of California Press, £24.95, ISBN 9780520262874

One benefit of the sheer bulk of each of these *Selected Poems* is that we can see how their authors' mature voices emerged through a process of casting-off. Various possibilities are re-assembled into a more consistent authority. Yet, having ploughed through hundreds of pages of work, some of it re-encountered, I must say that it can be an uncertain pleasure to have the opportunity to consider a poet's development in this manner. I wonder what benefit the publishers see in putting out such large 'selections'. If it is a question of bringing a poet's early cast-offs back into the picture now that eminence has been assured, presumably a more determinedly selective editorial approach might have been taken. If the ambition is to put back into circulation a plethora of out-of-print work for readers to enjoy – well, again, some more critically- or editorially-assured approach might have gained fuller interest and admiration for their authors. The old Carcanet *Poetry Signature* selecteds (c. 120pp.), and some of the Penguins, probably had it about right. These three books, two of which weigh in at roughly 250pp., and one at over 300, provide a bit much formative work to be re-encountered.

Given this, it is worth pondering why August Kleinzahler's work really comes into its own with the poems from the second half of his career. After all, much of the material and approach which underscore the achieved and compelling voice of the last two full collections is there in the early poems. Despite the suburban disillusionment and loneliness of its 'rapid' modernity, actually a lot of Kleinzahler's material strikes a plangently Romantic note, through its aubades, hymns to the moon, or various slow 'trances', in which we watch the flourishing of plants or trees. This is self-consciously the case in 'Sunset in Chinatown', where "the sun sits low" before

exploding

> suddenly in the window of Goey Loy Meats, high
> along the top of the glass,

> showering light over barbecued ducks –

> a somehow elegiac splash [...]

The disconnection between sunset and setting of the poem, and the generic connection ("somehow"), mark the unease in much of Kleinzahler's earlier work. This awkwardness is cultural as well as tonal; the surrealism achieved by the ducks cooking in the penultimate line quoted is immediately unnerved by the next line's "elegiac". Why, we are left to wonder, is that tone appropriate to Chinatown, why cite the name of the meat company, why "exploding"? The poem's voice cannot accommodate such a panoply of perceptions. The writing in the second half of the book, though, is the real thing. The voice is immediately declarative; partly, it seems, because Kleinzahler has settled into a more consistently satiric perspective, on both city and country, which integrates the traditional elements it continues surprisingly to harp on. There are some fine variants on Juvenal, for instance, which carry real assurance and delight, as in 'Epistle VIII':

> Accident, contingency: it's city nature, Maecenas, that's for me,
> not those endless manured fields, lowing cattle and whatever sheep do.

If Kleinzahler comes across as a poet hitting a stride, Glyn Maxwell's style is confirmed as having been established early in his career. The muddling-around with details from the everyday urban world, the casting of them into odd, child-like stories, is an approach taken from the first book to the most recent. Unplaced, enigmatic lyrics, which throw cliché into surprising contexts and tonalities, are established fairly near the start of this volume:

> Western Garden Citizen, I stand
> At midnight in the east and say, 'I'm lost'.
> But I'm starting to get to know the back of my hand,
> At the cost of moving on, which is no cost.

What's startling is that it is difficult to get any purchase on the voice, on the implications of what we are told. The book's many speakers, often unidentified, share their lostness with us in a variety of parables which bear a sometimes indeterminate connection to subject or audience. Is the "no cost" here anything more than playful? Has the poem earned the challenge upon which it ends: a sardonic "What have you got?"

These are numerous rehearsals of similar themes. The poems are most telling when – in a way almost equal to the best of Auden – they find themselves, as in the recent 'A Play of the Word', deploying ballad-like refrains and repetitions. Actually, therefore, the most surprising and compelling of Maxwell's work is that in which the address of the poem is directed and personal. The fourteen 'Letters to Edward Thomas' allow Maxwell to unveil, however ironically, the historical and national understanding, as well as the nostalgia, which lies behind the otherwise often airless parables:

> You
> Were land to me, were England unestranged,

> Were what I thought it had amounted to,
> But look at the fields now.

Michael McClure's politics were honed through the '60s and the Vietnam trauma; his poems' energy and unpredictability offer deliberate rebuke to the monolithic imperialist state. At this distance, the politics are also surprisingly exculpatory, displacing authority away from the individual whilst (prematurely for us in this time of Afghanistan and Libya), proclaiming the new dawn:

> The new civilisation will not be communism!
> POLITICS ARE AS DEAD AS THE CULTURE
> they supported!
> .....NEW SOCIETY WILL BE BIOLOGICAL!

The quirky centre-of-the-page lineation, and random shouty sloganising of much of McClure's poetry, does not reduce the fact that his organicism pays off with some intriguing formal inventions, especially in the more recent work. The various 'graftings' of the late '90s, for instance, show him remaking previous poems to new ends, a process signalled here by the chronologically-displaced poems from *On Organism* of 1974, with which this *Selected* opens. The paired poems of the early '60s, 'Ode to Jackson Pollock' and 'The Chamber: for Jack Kerouac', capture this most directly, especially when the former hymns the artist's method: "of making each motion / your speech, your love, your rack / and found yourself. Heroic – huge – burning / with your feelings."

Yet the most recent work included here is probably the most satisfying, testament to the metamorphic and continuing energy of McClure's writing. The sixty-five 'Swirls in Asphalt' are perhaps the most formally engaging, but also the most sympathetic of these works. Through a series of love songs in age, they recognise hard-won victories over circumstance:

> THE MUSIC IS NOT SO BRIGHT
> and the mind is deeper
> and the layers are ragged;
> at each frayed thread tip
> star chambers
> are woven with vernal flowers [...]

Steven Matthews's collection *Skying* will appear from Waterloo Press shortly. He is Professor of Poetry at Oxford Brookes University.

The Child Is The Mother Of The Woman

ALAN BROWNJOHN

Wendy Cope, *Family Values*, Faber, £12.99. ISBN 9780571227421;
Rita Ann Higgins, *Hurting God*, Salmon Poetry, £10. ISBN9781907057052

It was once possible to read reasonably happy family recollections done in prose. But misery memoirs, or at best rather curious and disturbing accounts of offbeat early years, are now what publishers, and readers apparently, seem to want. With poetry, though, things haven't greatly changed. It's still perfectly in order to write affectionately about lost persons and places, and indulge a nostalgia for happy experiences. On the negative side, feeling rueful and regretful and analysing a little guilt is about as far as it goes.

And that is where Wendy Cope's new book takes off, because the Christmas pieces at the beginning, agreeable but standard in form and sentiment, are no preparation for the succession of slightly weird scenes, impressions and anecdotes from childhood which follow. The family poems and problems start with 'Differences of Opinion', where a tense quarrel springs from having parents both of whom believe the earth is flat, and make that a matter of loyalty and religious principle:

> It's bad to make your mother cry
> By telling her the world's a sphere.
> It's very bad to tell a lie [...]
> It's bad to think your mother odd [...]
> All this has been ordained by God.

Clearly, not wishing to take communion (in 'Sunday Morning') or being "cross and sad" about departing for boarding school are also sins against mother, whose love is never to be questioned. Refuge is taken, touchingly, in the less possessive affection of the 'Daily Help', and even school eventually offers one humorous friendship protecting the poet-narrator against the bullying older girls who "decided / That I used too many long words". In a moment of characteristically deft wit Cope recalls that:

I soon learned not to.
Look at how I write.

As always with this poet, the simple, even wide-eyed, statements and relaxed treatment of any topic are deceptive. Cope has received the Michael Braude Award from the American Academy of Letters for light verse. The late Gavin Ewart also won it, for a lifetime spent writing very funny, frequently scandalous poems of immense technical accomplishment; it isn't given lightly, but as a reward for work of some substance. *Family Values* moves on from home – after recalling the African visitors who disappointingly turn out to be white, and the bus driver uncle who was barely permitted to call on the poet's mother – to equally plain and direct poems about a motorway service station with no more red plastic tomatoes full of ketchup on the tables, visits to Lissadell and Steep (remembering W.B. Yeats and Edward Thomas respectively) and a gallery of 'Dutch Portraits' which move Cope to unexpected tears. As in the family poems, the poignancy is in the lucidity. Yet Cope's ability to communicate lies as much in the unobtrusively confident handling of forms like the sonnet, the triolet, the pantoum and the villanelle. The thought of mortality renders her impatient, as much as anything else, in 'My Funeral', where Ogden Nash comes to mind:

> Though I will not be there,
> Glancing pointedly at my watch and fixing the speaker with a
> > malevolent stare,
> Remember that this was how I always reacted
> When I felt that anybody's speech, sermon or poetry reading was
> > becoming too protracted.

The book ends with extracts from two commissioned sequences, one written for the Endellion String Quartet and the other for, and about, BBC Radio 4. In these she jumps from topic to topic just as exuberantly as she did in the jokes, parodies and satires that first made her name in the 1970s.

Rita Ann Higgins's *Hurting God* similarly focuses on childhood at its outset, and, as the title suggests, explores similar tensions. But this mix of poems and short prose pieces – the book is subtitled 'Part Essay Part Rhyme' – naturally owes far more to Irish folklore, Joyce, Beckett – and Flann O'Brien – than to any English light verse tradition. Her mother is a poor villager pegging clothes on a line and polishing the altar for a "loving Godling". She is also a conduit for the detailed and disarming requirements of the priest (one poem is called 'The Priest is Coming We Can Feel It in Our Bones'), the nuns at the Poor Clares convent, and a God hurt by the people who favour "bungalows and washing machines and venetian blinds and tight slacks on women."

The rapidly changing working-class community in 1960s Galway is pulled in one direction by English and in the other by the nuanced attractions of the Irish tongue; Higgins's moving poem 'The Other Language' is offered in both, and ends:

> they were drinking in another language
> they were barking in another language
> they were arguing in another language
> and when all the talk came up about emigration
> they were crying in another language.

"I'm a disturber", this author declares. Her poems and essays build up a scary and yet entertaining narrative of growing up discontentedly into the employment world of "the multinationals" that come and go: "Our fag breaks / became our summer holidays / when the Big Boys pulled out." *Hurting God* is a volume in which, as Higgins wishes, "ideas come with a new crispness [...] words have a ping in their step [and] sounds evoke a memory that may be long forgotten." To be greatly recommended, it's a true poet's take on the bungalows and bail-outs of a modern Ireland, in which Yeats would applaud the writers but be sad to find a country for capitalist old men.

Alan Brownjohn's *The Saner Places: Selected Poems* is published by Enitharmon Press in July 2011; he received a Lifetime Achievement Award from the Writers' Guild of Great Britain in 2007.

The Shock Of Imaginative Liberty

W.N. HERBERT

Robert Hass, *The Apple Trees at Olema: New and Selected Poems*,
Bloodaxe, £15, ISBN 1852248971;
C.K. Williams, *Wait*, Bloodaxe, £9.95, ISBN 1852248009

There is an exhilaration about reading certain poets whose powers continue to heighten with age – their gifts have somehow conspired to coincide with their maturity. Some peak much earlier: an extreme case would be Rimbaud, while others, like W.H. Auden, seem made for middle- rather than old age. But the great poets of the later decades – Thomas Hardy and Stanley Kunitz come to mind – excite because the reader rapidly understands that their imagination can and will go anywhere. Robert Hass and C.K. Williams are barely septuagenarians, but both give off this shock of imaginative liberty in their latest work. Each can be said to have been cultivating just such liberty throughout their careers – each has been prolific, publishing around twenty or more books each – but in these collections there is a sense that they are not merely reconsidering, but are prepared to completely remake, the themes of their earlier work.

C.K. Williams's collection, his tenth with Bloodaxe, is in four restless sections, moving between the tensile line for which he is famous, and the shorter emphatic measure he put to such interesting effect in, among other volumes, *The Singing*. He also moves between lyric aperçus based in direct observation, variations sparked by a literary or mythic theme, and ruminative meditations on how thought becomes convoluted as it tries to engage with, and evade, its own limits. In each he displays a master's sure-footedness in shaping the poem and moving between the registers of sharp observation and sonorous summation. But he also displays a daring flexibility of register, as happy to plunge into italic emphasis as to invoke a god – sometimes within the same poem.

Wait's first section consists of series of responses, compassionate, subtle and precise, to animals and people, as they reflect each other and present themselves, whether in lived experience or in the imagined second life of reading. A fish-head on the pavement outside a "hairdressers' supply store" is a sufficiently odd conjunction to draw the observation that:

> It must recently have been left there,
> its scales shone and its visible eye
> had enough light left in it
> so it looked as they will for a while
>
> astonished and disconsolate

In contrast the heads in the window behind, "bewigged, painstakingly coiffed", are also anthropomorphised in what effortlessly becomes a meditation not on mortality, but on the Yeatsian theme of how we handle our awareness of mortality. The lifeless head and the simulacra ironically contemplate what they cannot, while the poem flips this over to challenge us and itself: "Better stay here, with eyes of glass, / like people in advertisements, / and without bodies or blood, / like people in poems."

This image of presence or its lack is explored in several other poems: a woman on the Paris Metro, glimpsing an affinity between what she and the poet are reading, "becomes *present* in a way she hadn't been before", the body responding to the mind; rejecting his youthful touch, a girl "began turning her belly to wood [...] the rest of her to something harder." That this is a species of metamorphosis – that metamorphosis is, itself, our way of explaining the interactions of our passions and our intellect – is underscored by a series of poems focused on reading (Marina Tsvetaeva, Annie Dillard, Ortega y Gasset), which counter any simplistic division between the life of the mind and that of the body. The estrangement between Coleridge and his son is reprised "as though he were a character / in one of the more than minor tragedies he might have written."

Missed opportunity, the persistence of guilt, and the recurrence of the unsaid, haunt a portrait series near the centre of the book: a mentor whose potential fizzled out in Mexico, Martin Luther King and Robert Lax, in an elegy which focuses on a point where the undone is in a sense accomplished, and the done incomplete: the act of prayer.

> And here Lax prayed, the way he prayed – no one really knew quite how he prayed – (of fishermen he wrote that one '...*crossed himself (lightly) without seeming to; the others not, without not seeming to...*')

That the lucid complexity of Lax's phrase appears absorbed within the poet's own intricately accurate syntax is a marker of capaciousness. There are plenty of examples here of Williams's characteristic line and its capacity to shake up the syntax with an unexpected word: "literally, with precision, and no patching of gaps with however inspired imaginative spackle." In the final poem, 'Jew on Bridge', heritage, identity, literature and responsibility are all confronted in an exploration after a brief passage in *Crime and Punishment*: "On page something or other, chapter something, Raskolnikov sees JEW." As with Tsypkin's *Summer in Baden-Baden*, what follows is an attempt to reconcile what is great with what is despicable about us. Ranging from family history to the deaths of Paul Celan and Walter Benjamin, Williams evokes the act of dying not just as "that moment you know you are going to die", but "the moment past that" in which we apprehend the marvelous pattern of our limitations as, in Celan's term, fugue:

> [...] the searing through you you realise is your grief,
> for humans, all humans, their world and their cosmos and oil-cloth
>   stars.
> All of it worse than your fear and grief for your own minor death.

Unlike any single collection, a *Selected* allows you to see time and experience in the act of boiling away what the poet considers to be unnecessary or less successful, and the distance across which – and the intensity with which – themes, lines and ideas recur in an imagination. *The Apple Trees at Olema* is a succinct summation of almost forty years' work, from 1973's *Field Guide* through to a body of new poems in which Robert Hass's typical concerns are subjected to new scrutiny, and his customary approach to these concerns are tested by this most stringent of imaginations. From that first collection he has been setting his exceptional eye for the Californian landscape against the sometimes cataclysmic intimacies of family, and has charted the changing demands of his passionate engagement with both the intellectual climate of the US, and the ruthless revisions of its history.

Present from the beginning is a lyric exactitude of vocabulary when it comes to plants, animals and particularly birdlife. Hass is a master of modern eclogue: "Toyon, old oak, and coffeeberry: always about halfway, / but especially if the day had been hot, the scent of vanilla grass". He has a way with couplet which he plays against the different tensions of the long poem or sequence in contrasting forms: "The dead with their black lips are heaped / on one another, intimate as lovers." There is the capacity to step into or out of the poem at a critical moment, to shift the reader's perspective on what is being done: "The woodsman and the old man his uncle [...] / have stopped working / because they are tired and because / I have imagined no pack animal". There is the light touch with intellectual complexity: "The snark is writing a novel / called *The Hunting of the Self.*" And above all there is the concision and memorability with which he introduces the major themes of public and private life, whether the late and subtle 'Bush's War' which both isn't and is about what its title suggests, or the intense domestic rites of passage of nurture, divorce, acceptance and bereavement which occupy four key poems, 'Santa Barbara Road,' 'My Mother's Nipples,' 'Regalia for a Black Hat Dancer' and 'August Notebook: A Death'.

In the first of these, the dialogue between father and teenage son, in which they are simultaneously separated and united by the act of reading and the particular texts they use to talk to each other, is handled with great subtlety, the son encountering Sartre and rebellion at the same moment as the father tries to engage with a form of classical Chinese poetry, the alternating rhyme and prose of *Fu*:

> 'Bullshit,' he mutters, 'what is the existential reality' –
> he has just read *Nausea* in advanced English –
> 'of all this bullshit, Todo?'
> Todo is the dog. It occurs to me
> that I am not a very satisfying parent
> to rebel against. *Like an unmoored boat*
> *drifting aimlessly, not even valuing*
> *the breath of life, the wise man*
> *embraces nothing, and drifts with it.*

Even as he ironically depicts himself using Chia Yi's ancient '*Fu* on the Owl,' Hass can't resist reordering the lines of the original for dramatic effect. The related theme of his parents' marriage and his mother's alcoholism, not engaged with till 1996's *Sun under Wood*, is announced in a slightly earlier poem as "what my parents in the innocence of their malice / toward each other did to me." This collection revives images from earlier books – the grim naming of Steller's Jay and how the Archangel Raphael cured blindness – and 'My Mother's Nipples' alternates the Stevensian register of lines like "Alors! Les nipples de ma mere!" with the stark prose which depicts a ten year old boy finding his mother passed out drunk in a park: "I suppose I wanted for us to look like a son and mother who had been picnicking, like a mother who had fallen asleep in the wry light and scent of orange blossom and a boy who was sitting beside her daydreaming".

Divorce, the third marker of division from the Edenic pastoral, is first hinted at in one of Hass's carefully-modulated portrayals of sex as an attempt to recover an impossible wholeness: "They are trying to become one creature / and something will not have it." In 'Regalia for a Black Hat Dancer', the accidental loss of the poet's wedding ring is set against a deep field of reference summoning up the range of ideas and experiences that find home in his work – Derrida's discovery of groundlessness, vacant niches in European churches, the empty hands of a carved Buddha, all handled with a combination of intellectual lightness and emotional intensity, before settling on a simple, disturbing, liberating act – eating baby chicken in a Korean market and wondering "if you were meant to eat the bones. You were. I did."

The reader's sense of engaging with the whole life of a gifted and various writer reaches its conclusion in the poems about the death of his brother, an apparently addictive personality who denied the troubling inheritance of his parents' marriage. While his elegies for Miłosz, whose work he spent so many years translating, have a rounded gravity, a sense of a life completed, there is here a contrasting acceptance of anger into the fabric of the 'August Notebook,' which begins by preserving a misprint, includes a solemn quoting of the blues, and preserves the note-taker's present moment, as well as the provisionality of his emotional responses, setting it against the form in a manner that sums up this most civilised critic of what we as a civilisation and as citizens do to ourselves and to others:

> I imagine he is in one of those aluminium
> cubicles I've seen in the movies,
> dressed or not. I also imagine that,
>
> if they undressed him, and perhaps washed
> his body or gave it an alcohol rub
> to disinfect it, that that was the job
>
> of some emigrant from a hot, poor country.
> Anyway, he is dressed in this stanza,
> which mimics the terza rima of Dante's comedy
>
> and is a form that Wallace Stevens liked
> to use, and also my dear friend Robert.
> And 'seemed peaceful' is a kind of metaphor.

Together with the poet Yang Lian, W.N. Herbert is editing *Jade Ladder*, an anthology of contemporary Chinese poetry, which will appear from Bloodaxe in 2012. He is Professor of Poetry and Creative Writing at Newcastle University.

A Classical Education

EVAN JONES

Fergus Allen, *Before Troy*, CB Editions, £7.99, ISBN 9780956107350;
Judith Kazantzis & Jacqueline Morreau, *The Odysseus Poems: Fictions on the Odyssey of Homer*, Waterloo Press, £10, ISBN 9781906742232;
Peter McDonald, *Torchlight*, Carcanet, £9.95, ISBN 9781847770912;
Robert Saxton, *Hesiod's Calendar: A Version of Hesiod's Theogeny and Works and Days*, Oxford Poets, £9.95, ISBN 9781906188030

The recording I own of Auden reading 'The Shield of Achilles' begins with a brief explanation: "This is a poem called 'The Shield of Achilles', which takes a theme from Homer, where, you remember, the armourer Hephaestos makes a shield for Achilles – at the request of his mother Thetis – on which you see the whole world and farming and various things going on". Whether anyone "remembers" or "sees"' with Auden or not, he then ploughs forward into a poem that undermines the Homeric theme (one would have to be familiar with the original to know that, but it is clear that Thetis isn't happy with the product of Hephaestos's efforts). Auden makes the memory/vision, through Hephaestos, contemporary, concerned with modern morality, anti-war. In this way, again and again, the rocks of Ancient Greece are turned over in the fields of our era: classical themes exposed to modern thinking. These four new collections are at work in those fields – and all deal with the rocks in different ways.

In 'Before Troy', the title poem of Fergus Allen's fifth collection, the poet is a witness, seated with coffee before events unfolding like the drama leading up to the war at Troy:

> Hey! from the top floor and its shutters smoke
> Writhes up and flames symbolically flicker,
> And out of the doorway runs Helen wailing
> With the rowdies rising up after her.
> 'Alexandrus!' she screams, and bares her breasts.

And then the drama stops suddenly, "Someone shouts – / Whereon they all relax and take it easy", part of a low-budget video, it seems, the scene now caught. Like Eliot's Tiresias, the poet foresuffers the inevitable event, living through the artificial moment that precedes the war at Troy. But, where Eliot specifies that his speaker is Tiresias, this isn't Homer speaking, as far as the reader can tell. There's an irony present in both references to myth, but Allen's is in a way subtler. This isn't Helen, the scene not Mycenae, and the connection to Homer is slight and slippery at best (the coffee and video camera make that clear). Yet, as in Eliot, mythical figures are removed from one context, perceived by the poet in another. What comes through is a playfulness, the dominant tone in Allen's collection, which also approaches the myths of Orpheus, Nausicaa, the Furies, and others, in similar manner.

Judith Kazantzis's *The Odysseus Poems: Fictions on the Odyssey of Homer*, a typo-ridden reprint of a book which first appeared in 1999, has less room for irony and play. It is, often as not, re-telling the story of Odysseus, filling in blanks or modifying the original: Athene refers to Telemachus as "her brat, her godson"; Penelope compares herself to Odysseus's other lovers ("I'm bundled in, cheek by cheek / with impossible fairy women / masterful and all-giving beyond / anything I ever did for you in bed"); Odysseus will not reveal where "beautiful-haired Kalypso" grows her loveliest hair "for all the world / to run its fingers through", and is himself "a mad old loony in Ithaka", massacring young men. But without irony, the moral judgment imposed on the characters by each other seems wrong-headed. Toward the end, Telemachus can't help but wonder of his father, "did he really stuff / a charred pine-trunk / through the eye of a one-eyed giant, again rocking on the lip, / again saving the men. / Where are the men?" Homer didn't have our irony, didn't question where the gods are concerned – and the gods are *very* concerned throughout his *Odyssey*. So, in Kazantzis, Telemachus wonders, he questions, as we modern thinkers might. Her book is like this, focusing – too much perhaps – on what Homer left out of personal and interpersonal relationships. While this might sound appealing (and at times is), it is also inauthentic.

Within Peter McDonald's *Torchlight*, the classical is metaphor for the contemporary world – and sometimes the personal. The middle of the book's three sections contains a masterful translation of the 'Homeric Hymn to Demeter', called simply, 'Hymn'. It is, in many ways, a poem about motherhood. And that this mother is a goddess is never taken for granted. The poem is religious in nature, offering explanation as to why the seasons change and whom to pray to when a loved one passes. The themes of 'Hymn' return in section three, in the brief lyric, 'Broken':

> Once I had lost you, you became
> a little girl and not a woman,

> a little girl who cried and cried
> in the dark, as your sobs carried
>
> across land and water; echoed
> through my own cries [...]

This could be mother crying for lost daughter, Demeter crying for Persephone: the tears and sense of loss connecting the two poems, singing back to part of the longer 'Hymn'. McDonald approaches the classical in this way without irony, but the translation suggests to the reader that his subject matter – even if twenty-six hundred years old – is continual and worthwhile, as we experience the same wonders and horrors our ancestors did.

Where McDonald offers a new translation, Robert Saxton's *Hesiod's Calendar* is a version. Saxton tells the reader in his introduction that he has "no Greek", and has worked here from two other translations. This is common enough practice. Where his differs most from other versions of *Theogeny and Works and Days* is in its form: Saxton's *Hesiod* is presented in eighty sonnets. As such, the whole is now episodic. This adds an intimacy and immediacy, especially in those sonnets of *Works and Days* addressed to Hesiod's brother Perses:

> O Perses, my brother, listen carefully.
> Work till Hunger can only wish you dead
> and till Demeter, revered and garlanded,
> loves you (as I should) and fills your granary.

The poem retains its instructional feel, however, and a side-effect is that at times it has elements of the manual: Step XXIV, 'Don't profit in disreputable ways'; Step XXVI, 'Don't be undone by a bottom-wiggling woman'. If anything is lost in this transformation, it's that the long poem has a goal it intends to reach, whereas the sonnet sequence doesn't, necessarily. At the final sonnet there's no sense the poem has reached a conclusion, and the sequence sputters out. Still, Saxton's is an admirable feat.

Canadian poet Evan Jones's second collection *Paralogues* is forthcoming from Carcanet.

Four Debutants

LEAH FRITZ

Anna Woodford, *Birdhouse*, Salt, £9.99, ISBN 978184471788;
Nii Ayikwei Parkes, *The Makings of You*, Peepal Tree Press,
£8.99, ISBN 9781845231590;
Hilary Menos, *Berg*, Seren, £7.99, ISBN 9781854115089;
Omar Sabbagh, *My Only Ever Oedipal Complaint*, Cinnamon Press,
£7.99,ISBN 9781907090196

If first novels are usually autobiographical, so are most first poetry collections. In *Birdhouse*, Anna Woodford goes back in her family history to when her grandmother connected with the unlikely man she married, an Austrian Jewish refugee whose parents had been killed by the Nazis and who somehow made his way to Britain and into her life:

> She unwrapped the rest of his life like a boiled sweet from her handbag,
> removed his name – the German name that meant
> he couldn't open doors for her –
> called him Richard, name for a man she might have married.

Though this is somewhat tongue-in-cheek, Woodford clearly loved her grandparents and seems to accept this complete renovation of her grandfather as life-affirming, rather than a travesty.

Many of the poems, particularly those about her family past and present – her parents, partner, children – her love lyrics and her elegies, are tender and yet spare. Like some other contemporary poets who were educated at strict Roman Catholic schools (Martina Evans and Angela Kirby come to mind), Woodford confronts the world anew, retaining a spiritual connection but devoid of catachised guilt. The twelve-line title poem in which she describes a clitoral orgasm is sheer bliss. It begins:

> You fiddle with the catch
> between my legs until my mouth
> springs open and I am
> crowing like an everyday bird that has
> entered the heights of the aviary.

As 'Birdhouse' is the first poem in the book, it would seem a hard act to follow for its intensity, accuracy and – yes – its beauty. Yet, while not all the poems rise to that level of ebullience, Anna Woodford's perfect pitch, control of suspense and capacity for surprise are everywhere in working order.

Nii Ayikwei Parkes also draws on his personal history in his first collection, *The Makings of You*, but his approach is more reserved. He seems to have taken the advice credited to his father in the short sequence 'One Against Three', and applied it to his poetry: "Reticence, / he said, is the best kind of defence". We don't know whether the lesson a boy has learnt in yoga class does, in fact, win the day:

> steel yourself and wait. I exhale,
> feel my blood pump – ferric and vital
> as the expression of a standpipe,
> then wait for the first boy to strike.

Parkes's poetry is cool and unhurried, as in the charming sequence, 'The Cut', which tells the story of two Sierra Leonese children, nine and ten years old, walking along a dangerous old railway line to visit the grandfather they've never met:

> We could be seen from the air, I'm sure,
> but who would dare fly so close to the sun
> when even the earth felt like a lick of fire?
> A day when the benign insane, abandoned
>
> to wander in circles tangled as their hair,
> knew not to emerge from the shade. Determined,
> we sweated in the glare, consuming the quota
> of shallow breaths to get us round the bend

Balancing narrative and verse, the poet draws the reader into his poetry with the story-teller's 'what-happens-next?' A fine example of this is 'Background', about losing a girlfriend to another man, which ends in a gentle wistfulness: "I saw you wipe your red lips off his lower lip, the day I went home / wiser and stood by my open window, looking over Bedford fields, / while the riddled curtain you loved to grasp danced like a ghost." However, Parkes moves beyond the personal into African history in the long couplet sequence 'The Ballast Series': "Our planked fathers drowned simply / because weight is whatever we keep inside." He has lived on three continents and in the West Indies, known both poverty and comfort. His poetry is sophisticated, eloquent and wise.

According to the biographical note on the cover of *Berg*, Hilary Menos runs an organic farm in Devon. One would expect earthy poems, and there are some, including 'Judgement', where Menos nails the specific jobs of men at an abattoir in five quatrains. She casts the slaughterers as angels:

> Danny angles his saw. His halo is blinding today.
> The tattoos on his arms leap like blue flames.

and ends the poem, crushingly, "If you want blood, / there is blood. If you want men, / here are men." But Menos has a light side, too. 'Siberian Sherbet' starts with mysterious "orange snow" falling on Eastern Europe, and the usual fudged (ooh!) explanation by a Russian official. Then "The Steppe looked like Frozen Mango Pudding. / The village of Pudinskoye had been Tangoed." And so forth... In 'Bernard Manning Plays Totnes Civic Hall' the chicken king laughs (all the way to the bank) at outraged protests. And the listed ingredients in a prepared 'Tiramisu' become a found poem. It works.

This is grown-up verse, able to take on the world. In 'Face of America' Menos uses a form she seems to favour: two stanzas of six lines each. In the first she describes Marilyn Monroe – "They had to sew her into the dress it was that tight", it begins – but then in the second stanza the poem opens out:

> Every now and then beauty steps forward.
> On a shell, a chariot, a podium. Rolled up in a rug.
> And for one brief moment time itself steps back.

Venus, Helen, Cleopatra... Anywhere, any era. That is the breadth of Hilary Menos's vision. But then we are brought back to specifics – and that poster:

> Then there's the fall, the war, the telephone call,
> the men in suits with white powder, dusting for prints
> and, up on a billboard, the face of America, smiling.

My Only Ever Oedipal Complaint by Omar Sabbagh is, as its title suggests, largely autobiographical. A British poet of Lebanese extraction, his verse takes us into emotional realms that English speaking writers seldom enter. Quoting Theodor Adorno, Samuel Beckett and Paracelsus among others (a page of Adorno's *Minima Moralia* prefaces the collection), Sabbagh dedicates the book to his father with a poem called, 'A Father's Love'. The final stanza reads:

> Let me remember him, immemorial
> as ringed time in a tree;
> let the echoes of his voice remind me
> the whole way home
> of where home is;
> and as my eyes turn to glass
> I'll lift them up to a father's love.

A poem titled 'Infidelity' is inscribed to his mother; presumably the 'I' is meant to be her:

> I told you a thousand times
> And then blew it to you with a final twist,
> Wrenched the winds from my guts, flexed my lips
> And horrified you with the scaling din of it.
>
> [. . .]
>
> You would not listen, you could not hear.
> And when later you talked of caring
> I thought of another, less stubborn ear.

This is strong stuff, honest and daring. A philosophical poem, 'Hunger For The Object Far From Home' explores the concept of family – "Family is not obedience, a blindness of rigor, mortal to the end. / Family, mine, is the way one's life bends / Out of perspective" – and then goes on to consider "Beirut – call it home – is the blue judgement seat". A song, apparently for a child, is inspired by a paragraph in Ermanno Bencivenga's *Hegel's Dialectical Logic*. The book's final thirty pages are mostly devoted to love poems, underlining Omar Sabbagh's bona fides as an English romantic poet. Modern, post-modern, whatever, he trenchantly belongs in that canon.

Leah Fritz's *Whatever Sends the Music Into Time* will be published by Salmon Press in April 2012.

Travellers' Tales

NISHA OBANO

Fawzi Karim, *Plague Lands and Other Poems*, versions by Anthony Howell
after translations by Abbas Kadhim, Carcanet, £12.95, ISBN 1847770639;
David Morley, *Enchantment*, with drawings by Peter Blegvad,
Carcanet, £9.95, ISBN 18476770622;
Nancy Gaffield, *Tokaido Road*, CB Editions, £7.99, ISBN 0956735904;
Kelvin Corcoran, *Hotel Shadow*, Shearsman, £8.95, ISBN 1848611429;
Norman Jope, *Dreams of the Caucasus*, Shearsman, £8.95, ISBN 1848611290

The work of Iraqi poet and artist Fawzi Karim reminds me of that of
the late Mahmoud Darwish: it memorialises friendships that now
belong to other times, before lives were bent out of shape by ideology,
war and exile. "I have no companions but the clouds scattered by the winds",
Karim writes in 'Four Variations and a Coda'; a line which resonates with the
Afterword in which he portrays friends in the forgotten Gardenia Café,
Baghdad, where an empty space at the table has been set for the deceased
poet Al-Husairi.

Karim's first collection appeared in Arabic in 1968, yet *Plague Lands* is
his first to be published in English. The poems belong to the Romantic
tradition and are in free verse, although the influence of Arabic literature is
obvious: homage is paid to al-Rumi, al-Tayyib and Abu Nuwas. Themes of
exile and the isolated poetic voice dominate, concentrated in recurring
motifs such as the oleander and the mulberry, the Tigris, nakedness and
death. Despite those friendships at the Gardenia Café, Karim felt uneasy in
Iraq. Born in Baghdad in 1945, he left in 1978 "to survive". Refusing to align
himself with either communist or Ba'thist ideologies, under the guise of a
two-week holiday he escaped to London. Ironically, there he was reunited
with the "oleander tree" of home, where "everything is [...] dark or else
hidden behind walls"; London brought "me to myself, to what is deep inside
me" ('Afterword'). Contrasted with the "light" of the mulberry which
suggests a transitory social world, in which ideas – like clothes – come and
go, the oleander (uprooted when the Ba'thists destroyed the poet's home in
al-Abbasiyya to make way for Saddam's palace gardens) is visceral, naked,
"hot with our uniqueness" ('Plague Lands') and reflects the inner voice of
the poet. This duality – the life of the poet, for whom home is "a body forever

in transit" ('The Last Gypsies') and his poetry, which "always departs" ('Plague Lands') – runs throughout the collection before landing at the door of something fine; here for example, 'At the Gardenia's Entrance' where a middle-aged man is waiting:

> Without wasting much time, I ask:
> 'Do you know when it opens?'
> 'The Gardenia Bar was my hangout before the war.
> I used to have my own corner there
> with my friends around me'
> [...]
> He stretched a hand out, holding a rolled cigarette,
> And I stretched a hand to take it
> And smoke spread, blurring the two men
> waiting at the bolted door
> On the sidewalk of Abu Nuwas Street.

Plague Lands is an important collection by a poet whose voice we should have been able to hear in English long ago.

Enchantment is the leading ecological poet David Morley's eleventh collection. Here, too, transit and time are resonant themes. The collection begins with forays into the natural world in which we become Other, as in 'Dragonflies' where the poet, having dived into the pool, emerges to see:

> at eyelash-level the whiphands of Common Backswimmers surge
> [...]
>
>   Then these
> sparking ornaments hovering then islanding on our shoulders
> each arching its thorax into a question: what is the blue
> that midnights all blue? How can crimson redden before you?

Morley takes us into prehistory in 'The Lucy Poem', and into the time of legends in one of the many travellers' tales in this collection, 'Hedgehurst'. The poet's isolation is also explored in 'Library Beneath the Harp', about the Roma poet Papusza (Bronislawa Wajs, 1908-1987). Papusza learned to read, something that was forbidden for Polska Roma women. Forced into an unhappy marriage to a harpist at fifteen, she wrote many songs concerned with *Nostos*, or the return home. When this meaning was manipulated by the poet Jerzy Ficowski, who used her poems to convey an anti-Roma message, Papusza was ostracised by her *kumpania* and spent the rest of her life in isolation before her death. 'Library' ends:

> *Bronislawa Wajs, can you still hear me?*
> [...]
> The doctor smiles. My tears begin
> falling in myself all for myself.
> [...]
> I approach the abyss with my husband's harp. I shall tell him about
> Papusza.

Is this perhaps Papusza's final Nostos? All the poems in this collection are concerned in some way with movement and survival, whether it is the search for the waterhole in 'The Lucy Poem' or a place to set up camp before the court order arrives in the travellers' circus poems. And for those of us who have built ourselves into cities, it is easy to forget the other worlds that exist beyond our walls. Morley's poetry evokes with enormous skill and sensitivity the many ways in which ecological changes affect our economic and social lives. Threat does not reside in opposing tribes, but in the disappearance of lives and worlds that are often unheard and unseen; held in a delicate balance before "water burie[s] its song" forever ('Lucy'). Nominated 'Book of the Year' in 2010 by the *Telegraph*, *Enchantment* is a profound and tender work which confirms Morley's place at the helm of British poetry today.

The journey continues in the other three collections under review here: Nancy Gaffields's *Tokaido Road*, Kelvin Corcoran's *Hotel Shadow* and Norman Jope's *Dreams of the Caucasus*. Gaffield follows in the footsteps of the travellers along the Tokaido road captured in Hiroshige's woodcuts. "I want you to connect the image / with the human story", the poet says at Shimada. Despite the beauty of this fifty-five stage journey from Nihonbashi to Kyoto, her poems tell of the ardour of the road, the pain of the departure and the longing for reunion. While Gaffield's exquisite and intimate portraits leave you touched, Corcoran's impressive collection straddles land and centuries, taking us to Greece where ancient and modern times collide, sometimes with curious results as in 'The Family Carnival', where the festival of Apokriatika is underway:

> [...] dancing uncle is pregnant with a balloon,

He leads his son the satyr with lopsided breasts,
and his daughter, Happiness, skips in circles laughing.

Jope's poetic lines meander through what is also partly a travel journal as he takes us through desert regions where "the silence of the footprint [...] can outlast one's life", across the Danube and then far north to Magdelenefjord on the north-western tip of Norway where the poet had hoped to "create a text that resides in the aftermath of text ... to leap like a diver from the end of one's final sentence on earth" with "words that express the absence of words"('It Seems a Pity'). Each of these five collections has taken this leap and we are the richer for it.

Nisha Obano is the Assistant Editor of *Wasafiri* magazine.

The Art Of Selection

DAI GEORGE

Lawrence Sail, *Waking Dreams: New & Selected Poems*, Bloodaxe, £9.95, ISBN 9781852248833; Paul Henry, *The Brittle Sea: New & Selected Poems*, Seren, £9.99, ISBN 9781854115249; Anne-Marie Fyfe, *Understudies: New & Selected Poems*, Seren, £9.99, ISBN 9781854115201; Mary MacRae, *Inside the Brightness of Red*, Second Light Publications, £8.95, ISBN 9780954693480; Harry Guest, *Some Times*, Anvil, £8.95, ISBN 9780856464256

A *New & Selected* can serve one of several purposes, depending on when in the poet's career it appears; in Lawrence Sail's *Waking Dreams*, Paul Henry's *The Brittle Sea* and Anne-Marie Fyfe's *Understudies*, we have the full range. *Waking Dreams* already hints at the variety and satisfying, cumulative weight of a *Collected* – unsurprisingly so, given that it is Sail's second such retrospective (his first being 1992's *Out of Land*, which welcomed him to Bloodaxe after a nomadic early career), and that it contains nearly forty years' worth of poems. *The Brittle Sea*, by contrast, spans a sleek twenty years. Gesturing equally backwards and forwards, it marks Henry's quiet rise as a major lyric poet while whetting the appetite for what is sure to be a very rich later career. Then there's *Understudies*, a mop-up of Fyfe's first three collections accompanied by a generous selection of new work. If it charts anything, it is Fyfe's recent progress from one type of observational poise to another: broadly, a move from the autobiographical sketches of 1999's *Late Crossing* to more filmic, less overtly personal new material. Beginning with the most recent work, it's an introduction, a sampler, as much as it is a retrospect. Fyfe often finds her strongest poems in the American heartland. Hinting at Muldoon's 'Why Brownlee Left' and the final scene of *Five Easy Pieces*, 'Interstate' tells of a woman splitting from her lover at a diner with the "half-eaten fries" and "remains of hash browns" still on the table. What could be a melodramatic set-up turns into a refreshing escape from personality.

Paul Henry arrived so fully formed with *Time Pieces* in 1991, and has erred so little from his signal virtues in subsequent collections, that *The Brittle Sea* reads as a distillation rather than a progressive overview. Favourite subjects are water and sleep, given formal shape through the gentle, rhythmic ebb and flow of the verse. Henry exploits the stillness of the single-line stanza beautifully, as in the opening of 'The Breath of Sleeping Boys' (from 1996's *Captive Audience*):

> Something is about to happen.
>
> Legs are crossed fingers.
>
> A cup falls from its handle.
> A wall crumbles into the road
> under the weight of a flower bed.
>
> In their dreams
> something is about to happen.

Rippling, uneven stanzas, end-stopped lines hovering around the three-beat mark, strange things happening to everyday objects: this is quintessential Henry.

From the outset this poet has taken an imaginative interest in being old. The first poem in the collection ('The Widows of Talyllyn') pays tribute to the miners' wives who "lived as needed, hid their strength, / survived the male, modestly". It is tempting to read *ars poetica* into these words: Henry's craft, too, draws power from modesty and hides its strengths in deceptive plainness. However, powers of consideration and empathy encompass limitations as well as talents: the poetry is full of exquisite tone but free from attitude and, occasionally, tension. This well-selected volume should endear him to many readers, both old and new, but one hopes that the next twenty years will see Henry increasingly disrupting his well-honed skills. 'Acts', the superb centrepiece of 2002's *The Slipped Leash*, might well show the way. It is a messy, anguished poem about the absurdity and fluctuations of long-term love; the "months of not loving you / when the plates we keep spinning / simply spin".

Waking Dreams has an arc that is missing from *The Brittle Sea*. In many ways, Lawrence Sail has arrived where Henry was from the beginning. Among his new poems, we have 'A Leaf Falling':

> The stem snaps off, brittle
> as a wafer – another sycamore
> half-star on its way to collapsing
> its yellow ribs on the ground.

The quietude and concentration of this stanza is very Henry-like, as is its careful embodiment of the subject: the feminine endings of the first three lines enact the leaf fluttering down before landing on the firm stress of "ground". But this beatific universality was not always present in Sail's poetry. Where Henry's career started with a compassionate identification with widows, Sail's earliest collection (1974's *Opposite Views*) is built around two poems that take the side of repressed youth in an adult/child divide. 'Death of a Child' is a dark parable about the dangers of mollycoddling, with the central figure forever staring out at a world "beyond the tidy garden ways" of his family home, until one day he strays "down the unfenced ways". He dies "boldly, with joy", drowning in a lake where his parents find him with "his eyes still bright, staring beyond their world". The next poem, 'The Return', a corrupted, foreshortened ballad about an adult revisiting his childhood home after the death of his mother, ends with a suicide in a ditch.

From these primitive, Oedipal narratives it is hardly a smooth transition to falling leaves. Sail's 80s collections are pivotal. In *The Kingdom of Atlas* (1980) and *Devotions* (1987), I detect a distinct (and understandable) crush on Geoffrey Hill. 'South Yorkshire' is a place where, "on every side / strictest codes enjoin the landscape." This Latinate abstraction jostles against earthy, Anglo-Saxon "stopcocks" and "bolted pipes" in a classic Hillian formula. The influence is even more pronounced in 'Allotments', which ends by sanctifying the title subject as "the last real estate of common prayer". Some of this can, of course, feel second-hand. However, even where his register is heavily indebted, Sail strikes out on his own by declaring a ready affinity for the quotidian world of allotments, snooker players and boxers. Learnedness has never been more readily dismissed as donnishness than in the last two decades. That Sail didn't respond to this trend by adopting an ever more recusant, obscure stance, but chose instead to enter into dialogue with a more colloquial, personalised poetry, is a real triumph.

Finally, we have two volumes that are not selected, but which nevertheless have differing, poignant relationships with the retrospective format. Mary MacRae's *Inside the Brightness of Red* is her second volume, written during a time of terminal illness and published posthumously. Fortunately, it requires no special pleading; it is vivid, galvanised writing that makes one mourn for the fact that MacRae's gift emerged so late in her life. These poems have a bracing tendency not to mess around, present in the label-like titles ('Winter Sun' and "Pomegranate') and in the deadpan first line of 'Notes, 1967', which simply reads, "My mother, then." Harry Guest's *Some Times*, on the other hand, is the second collection to arrive since his own *New and Selected* (2002). Appropriately, its great subject is recollection, and it artfully deploys poetic ambiguities to probe the uncertain, shifting terrain of a septuagenarian's memory. Particularly fine is 'Unnatural History', a complex, intermingled song of innocence and experience – the trick being that it conjures the painful aspects of both. The elderly poet returns to a scene of virginal, fumbling romance and proceeds to fumble with the memory, till he returns home and finds in his schoolboy diary a harebell: "dry, skeletal, possessing one less / dimension than reality. So like the past."

Dai George's first collection is due from Seren in 2013. His criticism has appeared in *The Boston Review* and *The Guardian*.

Silences

ALISON BRACKENBURY

Toon Tellegen, trans. Judith Wilkinson, *Raptors*, Carcanet, £12.95, ISBN 9781847770837; Harry Martinson, trans. Robin Fulton, *Chickweed Wintergreen*, Bloodaxe, £10.95, ISBN 9781852248871; Milan Djordjević, trans. Charles Simic, *Oranges and Snow*, Princeton University Press, $19.95, ISBN 9780691142463; Giuseppina Franco Tall, trans. Marion Tall Wilkinson, *Donna Ignota: The Poems and Life of an Italian Emigrant*, Tall Publishing, £14.99, ISBN 9780956697103

"My mother was silence." This is a rare moment of quiet in *Raptors*, a whirlwind of poems, each beginning, "My father", a fantastical account of a frantic family by Toon Tellegen. Judith Wilkinson's preface to her admirably energetic translations stresses the "strangeness and rawness" of the original Dutch, and the influence of his grandfather's Russian stories upon Tellegen's sequence. Its (highly calculated) sound and fury can be heard in the opening poem:

> My father
> moved heaven and earth
>
> heaven broke and the earth tore
>
> my mother came running along a platform
> threw herself in front of a train on a daily basis […]
>
> my father felt so cold

This remarkable series of simply-worded tiny epics is sustained by Tellegen's skill as a storyteller (his many other works include very popular children's books). Many of the poems play explosively with an initial figure of speech, for which Wilkinson has skilfully found English equivalents: "My father / was on cloud nine." Violent actions end with striking resolutions, each immediately undone by the next poem: "and my brothers threw him away. /// My father [...]". Tellegen's most disturbing themes may be the most familiar, such as his glimpses of parental sex; certainly, the poems' effect is as loud and continuous as life.

Tellegen compares *Raptors* to jazz improvisation. It could also be compared to opera. Just as Don Giovanni's exit leaves a gaping hole at the opera's close, the father's presence broods over Tellegen's final poem, which begins, with masterly patterning, "My mother". The violent presence *Raptors* has conjured still haunts its final lines as, "tousled" and confused, "my mother [...] thought of my father". The end brings silence, but not peace.

The sounds of Harry Martinson's poetry are brought to English ears by a helpful introduction by Staffan Söderblom and the inclusion of the Swedish text for key poems. As a young man, Martinson (1904-78) worked at sea as a stoker. Through the consonants of his poem, the "steam collier" clanks into our hearing, "*en koltramp komma*", and the battered ship's steam exhales: "*slickande sine sår*". Martinson senses the power of machines as a living force. The steam engine he rode as a boy is a "steel beast". But he also understands economic power. When he describes the "patient cable-fishers" mending the transatlantic telephone link, he quotes a shipmate who says the millionaires are "murmuring" down the line about "the lowering of our wages". His poems continually earn the quiet respect due to hard-won knowledge; that "Durham coal" powers a ship best; that a lapwing's eggs are "a little larger than those of a dove".

Yet Martinson's work has a dark reticence. His quiet 'Home Village' is "a silent lie"; there, he experienced violence then abandonment. He condemns "false" nature poetry where "the real truth about noise, pollution and destruction is stifled into silence". Unlike John Clare, he has a traveller's imagination (this selection includes part of his space epic). He can see the exotic in the familiar: a bat is "half of a tiny black umbrella". Observing chickweed, he salutes "the determination of the fragile". The strength and delicacy which mark this selection of his poetry and drawings are beautifully rendered by Robin Fulton's translations. Ageing, Martinson increasingly records destruction, such as the demolition of a cottage to which "silence had returned". But he returns to favourite subjects with a concentration so perfect it is an act of love, describing again, after two decades, the bat flying "soundlessly" with his "little flattened face". Though he slipped into silence after his controversial Nobel prize, Martinson's last poems come from a man who might fall out of love with words, but never his fragile, powerful world: "Too fine to be said flickers the wind".

Charles Simic's introduction to his translations of Milan Djordjević's *Selected Poems* wisely emphasises the background knowledge of a "native reader": "so much remains unspoken". Djordjević's unspoken background includes childhood in the (then) Communist Yugoslavia; maturity as a wartime political opponent of Milosević; post-war travel, then a near-fatal accident leaving him virtually housebound. The Serbian parallel text reveals Djordjević's frequent use of short energetic lines in (mainly free verse) poems crackling with exclamations and imperatives. "Show your hands! [...] I say this is heaven!" A poem in praise of bread ends: "Ah, the blazing silence". Erotic early poems cherish "afternoon silence". The work conserves an urgent richness:

> This silence is eternal and never to be repeated.
> She has the gentleness and softness of bird feathers,
> the bliss of October afternoons the color of honey […]
>
> as fresh as the taste of just-picked strawberries.

Djordjević is a poet who greets even misfortune with dramatic humour: "My dear Mr Accident". The poems after this 'meeting' are bare but intense descriptions, of the "tiny little life" of indoor spiders (and their prey). Recalling his travels – 'Clouds of Tuscany' – he approaches mortality with characteristic energy: "I sail toward my death […] disrupt my silence with your thunder".

Djordjević's work is a marvel: humane, passionate and tempered by experience. Simic's translations read beautifully and variously, by turns sensual and plain. His devoted attention should ensure that these poems are read internationally.

Donna Ignota (Unknown Woman) is also a labour of love: a bilingual memoir of an amateur Italian poet, Giuseppina Franco Tall (Pina), with prose translations of her poems by her daughter. I found it enthralling: proof that poetry, with its heightened vocabulary and recalling rhymes, is the echo chamber for the memories of family and community. (Family publishing of poems is a trend I welcome.) Ornella Trevisan, the editor, provides an absorbing biography of Pina, (1887-1952), the daughter of a Turin tanner turned factory-owner. Aged sixteen, she ran his company. She lost her brother to the First World War and her country to Mussolini, emigrating to London in 1936 with her English husband.

Pina's poems are steeped in song: the voices of girls in "the workroom's din", the "slow" songs of the tanners, the "incantation" of her mother's lullabies. A voracious reader whose education stopped abruptly, Pina did encounter poems by some of her famous contemporaries. Her verdict is thought-provoking: "I am too untrained for the new verse: it is affected, intricate and learned." Her own lines preserve her countryside's sounds: "At night martens rustled". She is highly conscious of salvaging the past. A tanners' outing is recaptured in a wreath of aromas: "the smell of tanning and wine mixed with smoke." A picnic near Turin, where the child Pina is allowed to play in her petticoats, ends with a song: "*Infine un canto*". But her poem's first line reveals that these fields were already lost to "modern blocks" in the 1920s. Among her darker visions, a poem about a 1933 Turin sporting spectacular quietly looks beyond the "blare" to the "coffin" of war. She hears the unspoken English hostility to immigrants: "You are too Italian!"

While the book's photographs trace Pina's progress from that petticoated child, its poems finally conjure an old woman "in the silent house", "her spectacles and the newspaper for company". "[I] grew up", wrote her daughter, "with the sound of these poems". *Infine un canto.*

Alison Brackenbury's *Singing in the Dark* (Carcanet) appeared in 2008.